Publishing and the Law: Current Legal Issues

Publishing and the Law: Current Legal Issues has been co-published simultaneously as *The Acquisitions Librarian,* Number 26 2001.

Publishing and the Law: Current Legal Issues

A. Bruce Strauch
Editor

Publishing and the Law: Current Legal Issues has been co-published simultaneously as *The Acquisitions Librarian,* Number 26 2001.

Routledge
Taylor & Francis Group
New York   London

First published by
The Haworth Press, Inc., 10 Alice Street, Binghamton, NY 13904-1580

This edition published 2013 by Routledge
711 Third Avenue, New York, NY 10017
2 Park Square, Milton Park, Abingdon, Oxon OX14 4RN

Routledge is an imprint of the Taylor & Francis Group, an informa business

Publishing and the Law: Current Legal Issues has been co-published simultaneously as *The Acquisitions Librarian* ™, Number 26 2001.

Cover design by Thomas J. Mayshock Jr.

Library of Congress Cataloging-in-Publication Data

Publishing and the law : current legal issues / A. Bruce Strauch, editor.
    p. cm.
    "Co-published simultaneously as The Acquisitions librarian, no. 26 2001."
    Includes bibliographical references and index.
    ISBN 0-7890-0777-0 (alk. paper)–ISBN 0-7890-0812-2 (alk. paper)
    1. Authors and publishers–United States. 2. Press law–United States. 3. Copyright–United States. I. Strauch, A. Bruce.
KF3084 .P83 2000
346.7304'82–dc21

00-053863

Publishing and the Law:
Current Legal Issues

CONTENTS

TAXES AND TORTS

ANTI-TRUST

ABOUT THE EDITOR

A. Bruce Strauch is Associate Professor of Business Law at The Citadel, Charleston, SC. He practiced tort law for fifteen years, has published numerous books and articles including works of fiction, and is the publisher of *Against the Grain*, the trade journal of the scholarly publishing industry.

Introduction

These are busy times for lawyers, and the blizzard of legal listservs could keep academe glued to the PC screen all day and into the night. To try to make sense of it all, we have gathered authors from academe, law firms and businesses to sort out four big areas of legal change that impact the scholarly publishing world.

COPYRIGHT

Copyright law developments are our lead as the biggest current legal issue in publishing.

Paul Gleason of the International Monetary Fund gives us a fine history of copyright law right up through current international treaties that struggle to deal with the electronic environment.

Norman Desmarais of Providence College develops the history of Fair Use and provides a practical guide to its application in the education industry. Of particular interest are his comments on the *LaMacchia* case and how it forced Congress to grapple with the inadequacy of pre-cyberspace era laws.

Continuing in that vein is *Leah Theriault* who worked for McMillan Binch, a Toronto firm of barristers and solicitors. She does a very thorough analysis of what she calls the Decline and Fall of Fair Use

---

A. Bruce Strauch is Associate Professor of Business Law at The Citadel, Charleston, SC. He practised tort law for fifteen years, has published numerous books and articles including works of fiction, and is the publisher of *Against the Grain*, the trade journal of the scholarly publishing industry.

[Haworth co-indexing entry note]: "Introduction." Strauch, A. Bruce. Co-published simultaneously in *The Acquisitions Librarian* (The Haworth Information Press, an imprint of The Haworth Press, Inc.) No. 26, 2001, pp. 1-3; and: *Publishing and the Law: Current Legal Issues* (ed: A. Bruce Strauch) The Haworth Information Press, an imprint of The Haworth Press, Inc., 2001, pp. 1-3. Single or multiple copies of this article are available for a fee from The Haworth Document Delivery Service [1-800-342-9678, 9:00 a.m. - 5:00 p.m. (EST). E-mail address: getinfo@haworthpressinc.com].

through (1) the judicial "Market-Centric" approach, (2) contractual override, and (3) new legislation on mass market licenses. Although she practiced law in Canada, Leah has an LL.M. from Berkeley and is quite at ease with U.S. Copyright Law.

Next on this topic is *Rob Richards*, University of Colorado Law Library. He explores the transition from copyright to licensing in the acquisition and use of information, gives us a contract law primer and the absolutely key elements of a licensing agreement. In a particularly good section, he outlines the perils of licensing where a contract grants a licensee fewer rights than those granted under copyright.

Legal research has come a long way from my youth when you went to a Westlaw index, located your case and then cited the volume and page in your brief. West was virtually the sole company in the business of taking public domain material and acquiring copyright through "sweat of the brow" and mainly a lack of challenge by anyone else. CD-ROMs and the electronic compilation and sorting of data begat *Feist* which has now begat the *Matthew Bender* case challenging West's copyright in its pagination system. *Ann Jennings* of InfoFacto–a legal research service–writes on this very timely case that is admittedly still in the appellate process.

Ron Thomson, Director of Publications of the Pontifical Institute of Mediaeval Studies in Toronto, discusses the impact of an incorrect interpretation of *Feist*. He sees a big threat to publishers of critical editions of ancient work and catalogues raisonnés who are having their works pirated by re-publishers of the data.

CONSTITUTIONAL ISSUES

Steven Anderson of Gordon, Feinblatt, Rothman, Hoffberger & Hollander in Baltimore, MD takes us through the ill-thought-out Communications Decency Act and shows us why the First Amendment makes it virtually impossible to regulate the Web.

TAXES AND TORTS (ARE WITH US ALWAYS)

Sheila Foster, Director of The Citadel's MBA program, lays out the tax deductions of the self-employed author, a matter of interest to anyone in academe who has a frail hope of actually turning a buck from the endless toil of scholarly productivity.

Your esteemed editor *A. Bruce Strauch* of The Citadel takes you through all the forms of tort liability that impact the publishing industry. He does his best to dispel the common myth that the First Amendment allows the outlandish fringes of journalism to operate with impunity. The First Amendment applies purely to government interference with the press. The English common law and more recent statutory product liability create very real limits on what may be put in print.

ANTITRUST

Under the current administration, once languid anti-trust law has become lively again. *William Hannay* of Schiff Hardin & Waite in Chicago writes about the collapse of the Reed Elsevier/Wolters Kluwer merger. Publicly-funded libraries were horrified at what the merger might do to their costs. Bill takes us through a brief history of U.S. Antitrust Law and the European Union Competition Law. It in fact was EU enforcers that caused the giants to back off.

Glen Secor of Yankee Book Peddler gives us a good look at antitrust law in the form of the Robinson-Patman Act with its prohibition of price discrimination. This is the operative law in the very much in-the-news bookstore suits against the big chains.

A. Bruce Strauch

COPYRIGHT

Copyright and Electronic Publishing: Background and Recent Developments

Paul Gleason

INTRODUCTION

Today's national copyright laws serve several purposes: (1) to guarantee an author a monopoly, or exclusive, right to control the uses

This article aims to discuss both the implications that electronic publishing has for the use of copyrighted works and some recent efforts made to protect such works from infringement in the electronic environment. It focuses principally on books and other printed publications, but much of the discussion is also applicable to other intellectual property products. Since discussing these complicated issues in a vacuum–without providing sufficient background information–is likely to be confusing and misleading to nonspecialists, the article devotes considerable space to explaining how the current copyright environment developed before getting into current issues.

Paul Gleason is Assistant Editor, *Finance & Development* magazine at the International Monetary Fund, 8101 Takoma Avenue, Silver Springs, MD 20910.

This article was first published, in a somewhat different form, in *Publishing and Development: A Book of Readings*, edited by Philip G. Altbach and Damtew Teferra (Chestnut Hill, MA: Bellagio Publishing Network, 1998). The views expressed herein are those of its author and should not be interpreted as reflecting the views of his employer, the International Monetary Fund.

made of his or her own (original) work for a specified period; (2) to guarantee a publisher a monopoly right to publish (or arrange to publish) and sell a work within national boundaries for a specified period; (3) to provide financial compensation (royalties) to authors to reward them for their creative work; and (4) to encourage progress in the country's arts and sciences (understood here to encompass the humanities and social sciences, as well as the "hard" sciences) in order to foster its economic, social, and cultural development. Edward Ploman and L. Clark Hamilton observe that "copyright is used as a legal mechanism for the ordering of social and cultural life, or, put another way, is one method for linking the world of ideas to the world of commerce."[1]

National copyright laws have often created, and continue to create, considerable controversy and rancorous disputes among authors, publishers, governments, and larger societies. In particular, the granting of a legal monopoly to publishers–which clearly has helped to provide them with sufficient confidence in their chances of recovering, through sales, their investment in editing, publishing, marketing, and distributing a work to justify their running the risks involved in almost any publishing venture–has conflicted with the reading public's "need to know" and its desire for the freest possible flow of information, with publishers' prices for books or other publications the main bone of contention. Such tensions have perhaps been inevitable because, although books, journals, or other traditional kinds of publications are physical commodities, each of which is sold at a particular price, the information they contain is a resource whose value to society is not diminished by the widest possible dissemination.

In their introduction to *Copyright: Intellectual Property in the Information Age*, Ploman and Hamilton explain that "copyright has become one of the most complex, technically difficult branches of law, an arcane area populated by experts hiding behind an almost impenetrable jargon."[2] Though it must be acknowledged that this branch of law has had to be designed to cover a wide variety of intellectual works and transfers of ownership, it is also clear that many influential book publishers and other major owners of intellectual property have long sought to protect their perceived economic interests by keeping national copyright laws and the relevant international treaties obscure and by dominating discussion of these by governments and international organizations.

Not long after the printing press was introduced in Europe, both secular and religious leaders, who clearly perceived the significant influence of widely distributed publications on public opinion, started to regulate the printing trade. They granted favored printers exclusive privileges to publish particular works and by this means were sometimes able to both prevent the publication of works they viewed as undesirable and to censor publications. In England, the political decline of the monarchy and the rise of parliament gradually permitted the book trade to have increased freedom of action, and the Statute of Anne–the world's first copyright law in the modern sense–was enacted in 1710.[3] Under the Statute of Anne, authors or any other persons, and not just printers as formerly, could own a copyright. The term of copyright was limited, and applicants for copyrights were required to comply with some formalities: authors had to register books in their own names and to supply free copies of each protected work (sometimes referred to as deposit copies) to several English universities and libraries.

In considering the Statute of Anne or later copyright laws, it is important to bear in mind that, as Ithiel de Sola Pool has so succinctly put it,

> The new notion of intellectual property represented by copyright was rooted in the technology of print. The printing press was a bottleneck where copies could be examined and controlled. . . . For modes of reproduction where such an easy locus of control as the printing press did not exist, the concept of copyright was not applied.[4]

Although copyright laws have come to cover many forms of intellectual property besides books over the past several centuries, the need to have a locus of control over the reproduction of works remains the paramount concern in copyright enforcement today.

During the remainder of the eighteenth century and the early nineteenth, copyright laws spread to the rest of Europe and the United States. International trade in books expanded rapidly, especially in Europe, and as it did so, the problem of international piracy grew. Piracy was rampant not only because of the quick profits it promised but also because intellectual property was still a relatively new concept. Although the concept of intellectual property and the idea that it was something deserving legal protection had gradually gained adherents, primarily in Europe, during the seventeenth and eighteenth centuries, attitudes toward works of the mind in some other countries were rather different. For example, in the United States, which adopted its first national copyright law in 1790, reprinting European (primarily English) works without either requesting permission or making payment was widespread in the 1800s. This activity was clearly piracy in the eyes of Europeans, but it was completely legal under U.S. copyright laws of that time, which protected only the works of U.S. authors.

EMERGENCE OF INTERNATIONAL COPYRIGHT CONVENTIONS

When printing-press pirates operated from a publisher's own country, the publisher could use its domestic copyright law to shut down their businesses and subject them to penalties; but when the pirates operated from another country, a publisher had no recourse unless the two countries happened to have a bilateral copyright agreement. European countries first made considerable efforts to negotiate such bilateral agreements on the basis of reciprocity of copyright protection, but the resulting web of such agreements proved to be unsatisfactory. Beginning in the 1850s, the idea of a common international framework for copyright protection emerged as the most promising solution. After many years of debate, agreement was reached in 1886 with the International Convention for the Protection of Literary and Artistic Works–more commonly known as the Berne Convention (named for Berne, Switzerland, the city where it was negotiated).

The Berne Convention, whose essential purpose, according to its preamble, is "to protect, in as effective and uniform a manner as possible, the rights of authors in their literary and artistic works," was designed to operate on the principle of *national treatment:* essentially, each member nation of the Berne Union (that is, a nation adhering to the Convention) will afford copyrighted works originating in *any other* member nation the *same* protection that works originating domestically receive under its own copyright law. The Convention provides that countries adhering to (that is, entering into a legally binding agreement to comply with) it must also provide a minimum standard of protection–in terms of the content, scope, and duration of copyright–to works originating in all Berne Union member nations. The

Berne Union, which began its existence with just 14 members, most of which were European, has expanded over the years to 125 members today.

World War II, which brought about many changes in the world publishing scene, marked the beginning of a new era in international copyright relations. The United States, which had remained aloof from the Berne Convention primarily because it wished to avoid the suppression of domestic interests that adherence was expected to entail, emerged as a major publishing power and began to take a greater interest in exporting books. It became interested in the development of a second international convention that would be acceptable to it, the nations of Latin America, and other nations that–mainly because they had so few works produced by their domestic authors and therefore wished to make works produced elsewhere as widely and cheaply available to their citizens as possible–did not wish to accept all of the obligations of Berne adherence. In 1952, the United Nations Educational, Scientific, and Cultural Organization (UNESCO) convened a conference in Geneva to work out such an agreement. The result was the Universal Copyright Convention (UCC), which came into effect in 1955. The UCC, which was signed by 40 nations in 1952, currently has 97 members.

DEVELOPING COUNTRIES CONFRONT
THE INTERNATIONAL COPYRIGHT SYSTEM

As the colonial empires of Europe broke up with the granting of independence to former colonies in the 1940s, 50s, and 60s, large numbers of new, often weak nations appeared and set about the business of fostering their own economic development. Although these nations' resource endowments, climates, infrastructures, education levels, and political philosophies varied widely, they generally agreed that they would need to obtain scientific, technical, and other information–much of which was in the form of copyrighted works–from the industrial nations if they were to realize their hopes for development. More generally, Third World countries sought to decrease their dependence on the information production and distribution system largely controlled by the industrial powers, since this offered hope of removing, or at least lessening, the fundamental inequalities between the two groups of nations.

As developing nations attempted to acquire more information from the industrial nations, the former's very limited means posed a major obstacle, as did the reluctance of many publishers and other producers of information in industrial nations to give up existing or potential overseas markets. In various international forums–including UNESCO, the administrator of the UCC; the United International Bureaux for the Protection of Intellectual Property (BIRPI), then the administrator of the Berne Convention; and the United Nations Conference on Trade and Development (UNCTAD)–developing countries, using their combined voting strength and enlisting the support of some sympathetic publishers and government officials in industrial countries, pressed for a lessening of their economic inequality with the industrial countries (the New International Economic Order) and, more particularly, a reduction in industrial countries' control of information production and distribution (the New World Information Order).

THE STOCKHOLM AND PARIS CONFERENCES

In 1963, an African copyright meeting held in Brazzaville (in what today is the Republic of Congo) first suggested that the Berne Convention be modified to give developing countries easier access to copyrighted works originating in industrial countries. This suggestion was pushed hard by developing countries before and during the 1967 Stockholm Conference held to discuss revision of Berne. After difficult and protracted negotiations, agreement was reached on a Protocol Regarding Developing Countries, which was annexed to the Berne Convention. At the same conference, the World Intellectual Property Organization (WIPO) was created to succeed BIRPI as the administrator of the Berne Convention. In 1974, WIPO became a specialized agency of the United Nations.

The Stockholm Protocol allowed several exceptions to the generally high level of protection provided to the copyrighted works of Berne Union members in order to assist developing countries. Among other things, it reduced the maximum term of protection of copyrighted works sought by developing countries; reduced restrictions on access to material developing countries needed for education and research; and provided for compulsory licenses–licenses provided by developing country governments to their domestic publishers in consultation with, but not necessarily with the consent of, the publishers or authors holding the rights–to translate or reproduce copyrighted works in return for what was considered equitable payment in the developing country concerned.

The Stockholm Protocol, conceived in controversy, failed to satisfy either developing or industrial countries. Most industrial countries refused to ratify the Protocol. Many substantial industrial country publishers, reacting to a perceived threat to their overseas markets, stepped up their efforts to protect the copyrights they held. National publishers' associations in industrial countries became more deeply involved in international copyright issues, as did the International Publishers Association, headquartered in Geneva. In addition, the International Group of Scientific, Technical & Medical Publishers (STM), headquartered in Amsterdam, was founded in 1968 partly to enable its members to better protect their copyrights.

Since the developing and industrial countries were stalemated in their dispute over the Stockholm Protocol, it was decided in 1969 that the best way forward would be to convene a joint conference for simultaneous revision of both the Berne and Universal Copyright Conventions. This conference, which was held in Paris in 1971, worked out revisions of both Berne and the UCC incorporating a compromise between industrial and developing countries on the latter's use of copyrighted works for nonprofit educational and research purposes. The Paris revisions, ratified in 1974, provide that publishers may reprint or translate works–subject to more extensive restrictions than had been included in the Stockholm Protocol–owned by copyright holders in industrial country members of Berne or the UCC. Developing countries thus obtained a significant, though limited, concession in Paris from industrial countries.

Despite the big head of steam behind compulsory licensing at both the Stockholm and Paris conferences, relatively few developing countries have granted compulsory licenses to their domestic publishers since 1971. Developing countries' wide-ranging campaign for additional concessions to help create a New International Economic Order and a New World Information Order subsequently encountered stiff resistance from conservative industrial country governments, especially during the 1980s, and was effectively, though not permanently, halted.

PUBLISHERS LAUNCH AN OFFENSIVE
AGAINST BOOK PIRACY

Book piracy continued to expand during the 1960s, 70s, and early 1980s as technological improvements in manufacturing and shipping, and strong economic growth in parts of the developing world, especially Asia, created many opportunities. While accurate figures on the volume of piracy are extremely difficult to obtain, it is clear that total annual losses of all copyright proprietors in industrial countries–including, among others, producers of films, videocassettes, audio tapes, compact disks, computer hardware and software, and books–from piracy of their works were, and still are, quite substantial.

Industrial country publishers, which had long been concerned about piracy and its effects on their balance sheets, became sufficiently alarmed by its magnitude during the early 1980s to push for, and obtain, strong action by their conservative, pro-business governments to combat piracy. The United Kingdom negotiated with several Asian nations known to harbor major producers of pirated books, videocassettes, films, computer software, etc., in order to win amendments in, and improved enforcement of, their copyright laws. At the urging of the International Intellectual Property Alliance (which includes the Association of American Publishers among its members) and other knowledge industry representatives, the U.S. government used the leverage created by the trade preferences and foreign aid it grants developing countries to convince such major pirate bases as Taiwan, Korea, Singapore, Malaysia, Indonesia, and the Dominican Republic to bring their copyright laws into conformity with the two major conventions and to beef up both enforcement of, and sanctions for violators under, these laws.

New legal provisions, particularly those enacted as a result of diplomatic and commercial pressure from overseas, have not always been energetically or effectively enforced but, on balance, considerable progress has been made against book piracy in developing countries. Such piracy is now widely seen as declining, though far from eradicated. At the same time, however, industrial countries clearly are becoming increasingly concerned about piracy in the countries of Eastern and Central Europe, as well as the states of the former Soviet Union, as their socialist economies and legal systems come to resemble those of Western Europe.

Many industrial country publishers recognize, however, that piracy can only be minimized or eliminated over the long haul by reducing the economic incentives that brought the pirates into publishing in the first place. In recent years, publishers in the industrial world have responded to piracy (including illegal photocopying as well as traditional printing-press piracy) and compulsory licensing by making greater efforts to sell their own books in developing countries at affordable prices and to sell reprint and translation rights–that is, to sell negotiated (voluntary) licenses–more reasonably than they had in the past. Nonetheless, conflicts between the interests of the industrial country publishers and developing countries clearly remain.

As printing-press piracy has diminished, the knotty problem of unauthorized photocopying of copyrighted works in developing countries received greater attention. In developing countries, as in industrial countries, the reproduction of copyrighted material without permission or payment is commonplace. Indeed, after many years of having had the freedom to make copies for personal or commercial use, many individuals and firms have come to consider such copying a personal right. The losses of income sustained by publishers whose books have been copied have been significant, though it should be pointed out that the combined losses to publishers from printing-press piracy and illegal photocopying have been dwarfed by copyright holders' losses from the piracy of such products as audio tapes, videocassettes, compact disks, and computer software.

Industrial country publishers, with finite resources at their disposal, have had to concentrate most of their anti-piracy efforts abroad on combating printing-press piracy rather than the much more frequent but smaller-scale photocopying infringements. Nonetheless, as an extension of their efforts to control unauthorized photocopying in their home markets through national collecting agencies, also known as reproduction rights organizations (RROs) (e.g., the Copyright Clearance Center in the United States, the Copyright Licensing Agency in the United Kingdom, VG Wort in Germany, Kopinpor in Norway, and CEDRO in Spain) set up to collect royalties for the reproduction of copyrighted works, industrial countries have set up the International Federation of Reproduction Rights Organizations (IFRRO).

As publishers and RROs have attempted to grapple with the photocopying problem nationally and internationally, many–though not all–industrial country publishers have concluded that charging users–especially large, institutional ones–on a transactional basis–that is, charging them individually for each copy made–is not feasible and that, consequently, collectively licensing large users–that is, charging them a fixed license fee for all of their copying (strictly speaking, only the copying of those works for which rights are administered by the RRO) during a specific period–is the only practical way to collect royalties.

While industrial country governments and their publishers have stepped up their efforts to combat book piracy in recent years, the economic and social development of some developing countries and the advancement of their publishing industries have induced them to change their attitudes toward the international copyright system. When a country reaches the point where it has substantial numbers of copyrights of its own authors and publishers to protect, it often becomes convinced that joining and strictly adhering to international conventions are in its own best interests. Among other countries, Korea, Taiwan, and the members of the Association of Southeast Asian Nations (ASEAN) have recently shifted their stances on international copyright issues for similar reasons.

EFFORTS TO INCLUDE INTELLECTUAL PROPERTY IN THE GATT

In addition to their increased direct efforts to combat piracy over the past decade, industrial country publishers–which have grown increasingly impatient with what they view as weak enforcement and inadequate protection of their rights under Berne and the UCC–have persuaded their generally conservative governments, many of which were impressed by the contributions made by copyright industries to their countries' export earnings and some of which viewed copyright concessions granted to developing countries as inappropriate international welfare schemes, to press in new international forums for better protection of copyrighted works. These efforts can be viewed as part of a larger trend toward industrial countries attempting to hold international organizations on a tighter rein than formerly and to use these organizations more deliberately to pursue their own, sometimes rather narrowly defined (national) economic and political interests. During the protracted (eight-year) Uruguay Round of multilateral trade negotiations that took place under the General Agreement on Tariffs and

Trade (GATT), which has its headquarters in Geneva, they worked to arrange inclusion of works of intellectual property for the first time. While developing countries and their publishers increased their involvement in the international copyright system over the past couple of decades, they generally resisted the proposed spreading of international copyright jurisdiction to encompass not only WIPO and UNESCO but also the GATT, primarily because they feared that the GATT dispute-settlement mechanism would be used against them, with the consequence that their access to the copyrighted works of industrial countries would be further restricted.

In April 1994, the Uruguay Round negotiations were formally concluded in Marrakech, Morocco with the signing of the Final Act by representatives of more than 120 countries. After receiving approval from enough participating countries' legislatures, the Final Act came into effect in January 1995. When the Final Act came into effect, publishers (and other owners of intellectual property) from industrial countries won inclusion of provisions improving the protection of the intellectual property they own. In copyright matters, the agreement essentially requires all participants to comply with the substantive provisions of the Berne Convention. Participants must provide procedures under their domestic laws to ensure that intellectual property rights can be effectively enforced by both their own citizens and foreign rights holders. The agreement also set up a Council for Trade-Related Aspects of Intellectual Property Rights, more commonly known as the TRIPS Council, to monitor the agreement's operations and governments' compliance with it. Any disputes concerning intellectual property rights are dealt with under the dispute-settlement procedure of the World Trade Organization (WTO), the organization that succeeded the GATT when the Final Act came into effect.

At this writing, it seems that copyright holders from the major industrial countries have, through their strong influence on their government's negotiators, wrested important concessions from users of intellectual property in developing countries. It will not be possible to know how international flows of copyrighted materials will actually be affected, however, until more experience is gained with application of the Final Act's provisions and the use of the WTO's dispute-settlement mechanism. Thus far, only a few cases concerning copyrighted intellectual property have been brought to the WTO's Dispute Settlement Body, and none of these have yet been settled.

PUBLISHERS' CONCERNS ABOUT COPYING

Publishers of books and other printed works, especially those engaged in scholarly or professional publishing, have seen widespread use of the photocopier considerably shrink the size of the markets for their works over the past several decades. They have often reacted, where competitive conditions have permitted, by raising prices of their works in an effort to maintain their earnings. Most publishers have survived, and some have prospered, during the photocopying revolution, and their efforts to combat unauthorized photocopying have met with some success. Nonetheless, they have found the experience to be profoundly disturbing.

Photocopying has clearly threatened to undermine the economic foundation of publishers' businesses in a way that no earlier technology had. With the printing press no longer serving as a control point for copies of a work, copyright enforcement became much more difficult, and many readers, businesses, and other institutions felt no compunction about making large numbers of copies of all or parts of books or journals, reasoning–to the extent they considered the economic and other issues involved–that publishers would make sufficient profit on copies sold through traditional distribution channels. Among publishers, some were inclined to attribute unauthorized copying to a moral deficiency among users and many called for stepped-up efforts to educate the public about the economic, legal, and moral justifications for copyright.

Although some readers and many of the librarians that serve them are convinced of the justification for payment of royalties on copies made of copyrighted works, most readers have neither considered the relevant issues nor been persuaded of the value of respecting copyrights. In such circumstances, many publishers, especially those in commercial publishing, have felt backed against the wall and have tended to view their customers (in the aggregate) with suspicion and mistrust, which has made true dialogue between publishers and readers hard to conduct and reasonable compromises very difficult to reach.

Many of the leaders of the publishing profession–especially in the United States, Europe, and other industrial countries–and their professional associations have therefore become convinced they can hope to survive in the new world of electronic publishing, in which copying has become far easier than in the print-on-paper world, only if radical new measures to protect copyrighted works are enacted and enforced. Not surprisingly, they have advocated the pursuit of single-minded, hardball approaches to achieving this goal.

TENSIONS OVER FAIR USE

Since an important purpose of copyright laws is to encourage the progress of a country's arts and sciences, there has and continues to be a need for people to be able to use portions of copyrighted works for free toward this end. The concept of permitting such use under the law, which is known as "fair use" in the United States and "fair dealing" in the United Kingdom, has its origins in English law and was established in the United States by various court decisions (case law) which gradually, though somewhat erratically, increased its extent. It was formally incorporated into U.S. statutory law with the coming into effect of the current Copyright Act in 1978.

Section 107 of the Copyright Act, which covers fair use, reads as follows:

Notwithstanding the provisions of sections 106 and 106A [which list copyright owners' exclusive rights], the fair use of a copyrighted work, including such use by reproduction in copies or phonorecords or by any other means specified by that section [sic], for purposes such as criticism, comment, news reporting, teaching (including multiple copies for classroom use), scholarship, or research, is not an infringement of copyright. In determining whether the use made of a work in any particular case is a fair use the factors to be considered shall include–

1. the purpose and character of the use, including whether such use is of a commercial nature or is for nonprofit educational purposes;
2. the nature of the copyrighted work;
3. the amount and substantiality of the portion used in relation to the copyrighted work as a whole; and
4. the effect of the use upon the potential market for or value of the copyrighted work.

The fact that a work is unpublished shall not bar a finding of fair use if such finding is made upon consideration of all the above factors.

The importance of fair use in the production of new works of the mind has been profound, since it has facilitated intellectual, cultural, and economic growth. At the same time, because fair use has threatened to diminish publishers' ability to earn a profit on the sale of their books or other printed works (although it has also benefited them in another way by facilitating the creation of new works), they have generally viewed it warily and have tried, through legal action, to keep its boundaries from expanding. Once the photocopier became commonplace, thereby facilitating inexpensive copying of larger portions of works than had previously been practical, their concerns about losing control of their intellectual property–owing primarily to fair use but also to other free uses of copyrighted works permitted by the Copyright Act, such as library copying carried out for various specific purposes–were considerably heightened.

Against this background, the arrival of electronic publishing technologies has made many publishers fearful that the greatly enhanced ability of users to copy digital works–and to make copies that are visually indistinguishable from the electronic original–would make the application of fair use and other exceptions to publishers' exclusive rights in copyrighted works an invitation to economic disaster. They have therefore sought to either eliminate fair use or reduce its scope in the electronic environment by both formulating the terms of licensing (contractual) arrangements with their customers and enacting changes in copyright law to accomplish this.

ELECTRONIC PUBLISHING'S IMPACT

When the Internet was originally used principally for electronic-mail exchanges and file transfers among scholars and, later, also for publication of textual information (without graphics) on gopher sites, there were only a limited number of users and almost all of the information exchanged was noncommercial in character. The attitudes of Internet users generally reflected the cooperative ethic of scholarly communication, with information sharing commonplace and unrestricted access to information widely encouraged. In recent years, however, the increasing popularity of the Internet, both for e-mail exchanges and for obtaining access to information published on the World Wide Web that is readable using graphical browser software (Netscape Navigator, Microsoft Internet Explorer, Mosaic, and others), has brought commercial concerns–and, with them, copyright issues–to the fore.

The ease with which the new technologies allow copies to be made of information published electronically (digitally)–on the Web, through electronic bulletin boards, from proprietary databases, and so on–and then downloaded to a user's personal computer and transmitted by a user to other users' PCs has been a boon to both scholarly and commercial communication and a cause of serious concern to publishers and other owners of intellectual property. On the one hand, owners of copyrighted information are attracted by the large audiences they can reach by publishing and distributing their works electronically; on the other hand, as was discussed earlier, they are alarmed by the risks of information being obtained by many users without permission or payment. For their part, many information users–and especially those in developing and transition countries and their governments–wish to obtain the maximum benefit from the new publishing and communications technologies but are very concerned that they will be prevented from doing so by the costs of not only the equipment and training required but also the charges copyright owners have levied, and may levy, for the use of information.

At the same time, both the scholarly community–in the humanities as well as the sciences–and the manufacturers of electronics and communications equipment and various providers of telecommunication services, such as telephone companies and Internet service providers (ISPs), strongly support the broadest possible access of users to information by electronic means. Although there is doubtless some risk in making statements about the views of general publics in various countries on these issues, because of their great diversity and the varying degrees of individuals' awareness of the relevant issues, it is clear that they also favor broad access to electronic information. The diverse views of the affected parties have thus set the stage for a replaying–in, it is to be hoped, a less strident form–of the debate on the uses of copyrighted works in printed form (described earlier) that created considerable controversy during the 1960s and 70s.

Over the last several years, both individual publishers and their national and international associations have put considerable effort into developing technical means to ensure their control over copyrighted information in electronic form. They have sought to develop electronic rights management systems (ERMSs) to monitor and license interactive uses of copyrighted material–that is, uses made of such material for which users choose when and where they will receive it. Publishers' efforts to "brand" their copyrighted material–embedding digital codes in it that enable the publisher to keep track of who uses it and to require payment, if the publisher wishes to do this, before the material can be used (for example, requiring receipt of payment before making encrypted material readable)–in this way have resulted in the creation of various systems, some of which are currently being tested as pilot projects. The basic concept these systems seek to establish in the electronic environment, then, is transactional licensing–that is, customers pay for each use made of the copyrighted material made available to them.[5]

In an electronic environment where many publishers fear that blanket licensing arrangements will offer them insufficient protection against unauthorized and uncompensated uses of their intellectual property, they are embracing ERMSs eagerly. For instance, at the most recent annual Frankfurt Book Fair in October 1997, demonstrations of the digital object identifier (DOI) system, an ERMS that has been developed under the sponsorship of the Association of American Publishers and more recently has been supported by the International Publishers Association, won glowing praise from publishers, especially those specializing in scientific, technical, and medical (STM) subjects. Dietrich Götze, chief executive of Axel Springer Verlag, described the development of such systems as "one of the most important events in publishing for this century," and Gerhard Kurtze, president of the Borsenverein (the German publishers association), termed it "surely the most significant structural shift in academic and scientific publishing since Gutenberg."[6] It seems clear that such effusive praise stems partly from an anxiousness to see ERMSs be adopted as widely and as quickly as possible to ensure protection of publishers' interests.

Electronic management systems pose some serious problems, however, and their widespread implementation is far from certain. For one thing, they raise serious privacy questions: will users of copyrighted works find it acceptable for copyright owners or some national or international administering body acting on their behalf to know what material they are using, as well as when and where they are using it? For another, the system of "pay per view" for copyrighted works in digital form that ERMSs could make possible would be unlikely to allow users any of their fair use rights. A third difficulty ERMSs are quite likely to face if they are extensively used is the devising of electronic means of getting around them–of allowing users to gain unauthorized access to information in which the publishers' digital codes are embedded. In the United States, the Association of American Publishers and other groups of intellectual property owners have been lobbying hard to make attempting to defeat ERMSs a violation of U.S. copyright law (discussed later on).

Interestingly, these potential difficulties with ERMSs are quite similar to those that arose a couple of decades ago when publishers attempted, with little success, to find a way to control the photocopying of their printed works by various technological means, such as the legally mandated installation of usage meters in photocopiers and the creation of special papers on which text could not easily be photocopied. More recently, though, a change made in U.S. copyright law has specifically prohibited efforts to import, manufacture, or distribute any device whose primary purpose is to defeat mechanisms designed to prevent copies of sound recordings (which have traditionally enjoyed less extensive protection under the Copyright Act than other types of copyrighted works) from being made by digital audio devices. Also, the (U.S.) Communications Act–which is formally outside copyright law–places similar prohibitions on devices that could be used to permit unauthorized decryption (unscrambling) of satellite signals carrying cable television programming.

It is clear that publishers need some form of special protection for their copyrighted works if their businesses are to remain economically viable in the electronic environment, but their need for this will presumably have to be carefully weighed against the need to maintain the public's fair use rights in this context.

NEGOTIATION OF NEW WIPO COPYRIGHT TREATY

In December 1996, after several years of discussion, negotiations on a new WIPO treaty intended to adapt international copyright practices to the new world of digital technologies and communication were completed in Geneva. These negotiations were controversial, especially in their final stages, as a result of the fundamental disagreements between some of the major industrial country governments and copyright owners, on the one hand, and an ad hoc alliance of developing country governments and the various groups of opponents in industrial countries (mentioned above) of copyright owners' plans to extend their control over uses made of works they publish in digital form, on the other hand.

In a somewhat unexpected turn of events, the copyright owners and their governmental supporters–led by representatives of the United States (whose delegation was led by Bruce Lehman, Assistant Secretary of Commerce and Commissioner of Patents and Trademarks) and the European Union–were soundly defeated in many of their efforts to get agreements passed to enhance their control over works they publish in digital form. Interestingly, the strategy of the U.S. delegation had apparently been to take the strongly pro-publisher provisions contained in *Intellectual Property and the National Information Infrastructure*–the report (more commonly known as the "White Paper") prepared by the interagency Working Group on Intellectual Property Rights, whose legislative recommendations had generated little enthusiasm or action in Congress after its publication in September 1995–and bolster their chances of enactment by incorporating them, with the help of their European and other industrial country allies, into the WIPO Copyright Treaty. Once the treaty had been negotiated by national delegates in Geneva, it was felt, this would create a sense of obligation in Congress to support passage of implementing legislation.

During the conference negotiations, attempts to make an incidental copy of a digital work produced in the random access memory (RAM) of a user's computer–by, for example, downloading a page from a copyrighted Web page–subject to the control of the copyright owner failed, as did efforts to eliminate for digital works the "fair use" exceptions to copyrights owners' rights that are currently provided for under various national copyright laws. Copyright owners and their supporters' efforts to make intermediaries in the transmission of digital works (for example, Internet service providers) liable for copyright infringements by their customers–to force them to serve, in effect, as copyright police–also failed.[7]

Various improvements in the protection of copyrighted works were, in fact, enacted in the treaty: for example, the applicability of Article 9 of the Berne Convention, which covers reproduction rights in copy-righted works and permissible exceptions to these, to digital works was clearly spelled out; the scope of protection for computer programs and original databases, and intellectual property owners' right of rent-al were clarified; it was made clear that infringement of any right covered by the treaty or the Berne Convention covers both copyright owners' exclusive rights and their rights to be remunerated for uses made of their works; the duration of copyright protection of photo-graphic works was extended from 25 to 50 years; and–perhaps most significantly–signers of the treaty committed themselves to provide legal remedies to penalize persons who attempt to circumvent ERMS technologies designed to protect copyrighted electronic works.[8] None-theless, what didn't go into the new WIPO treaty was considerably more important than what did.

The treaty has now gone out to WIPO's member countries for ratification and any amendments of their domestic copyright laws that may be necessary to bring them into compliance with the treaty's provisions. As of May 25, 1998, 51 countries had signed the treaty–in-cluding the industrial countries of North America and Europe but excluding Japan, Russia, China, India, Brazil, Australia, and most countries of Africa–and only two, Indonesia and Moldova, had ratified it.[9] On May 14, 1998, the U.S. Senate passed implementing legislation for the WIPO Copyright Treaty that included provisions mandating penalties for manufacturing or selling devices designed to circumvent ERMSs but also providing exemptions to nonprofit libraries, archives, and educational institutions to permit them to make acquisitions deci-sions and to computer software designers to permit them to engage in some forms of "reverse engineering" (analyzing software or another device to see how it works, with a view to creating a new device that can accomplish the same or a similar result in a somewhat different way). As of this writing (June 1998), the House of Representatives is currently considering similar legislation, with heavy lobbying ex-pected by publishers, software firms, online service providers, li-braries, educators, and their respective national associations. It is clear the U.S. ratification by the United States, through passage of this implementing legislation, would give a boost to ratification efforts by other countries that have signed the treaty.

At the December 1996 diplomatic conference at which the WIPO Copyright Treaty was agreed upon (as was the WIPO Performance and Phonograms Treaty, which will not be discussed here), a draft treaty on intellectual property in non-original databases, which was supported by intellectual property interests and their governmental supporters but opposed by numerous other groups including many from the international educational and scientific communities, was presented. Owing to the controversy over it and the lack of time available to consider the implications of the *sui generis* protection of databases (that is, a right of ownership in databases that would be inherent, regardless of their originality, which is seen by its advocates as justified by the work done and expenditures incurred by their proprietors in assembling and maintaining them) it called for, however, the treaty was put aside for subsequent consideration.

In September 1997, WIPO held a three-day information meeting on intellectual property in databases in Geneva. It was characterized by wide-ranging discussions of the subject, and, in the words of the report adopted by the meeting:

> Many delegations stated that they needed more time for further study and consultations on national, regional and international level [sic], and they stated that they needed further analysis to assess the need for such a system; furthermore these delegations pleaded for caution and [a] slower pace for international deliberations.[10]

The meeting therefore decided that the International Bureau of WIPO should thoroughly consider the discussions held at the information meeting and the issues raised, accept further submissions on relevant topics from member governments and other interested parties, and report back to its member countries on these by September 1998. Because of the preliminary stage of debate, no date was set for a future WIPO meeting on intellectual property in databases.

OUTLOOK

Given publishers' continuing fears about their economic viability in the electronic environment, they are likely to use their considerable financial resources and tight, sophisticated organization to continue lobbying strenuously, in concert with other groups of intellectual property proprietors, for better protection of the copyrighted works they own. Among other things, they can be expected to avail themselves of opportunities created by legal changes enacted in other countries–sometimes with U.S. publishers' offstage support–or in international treaties to upgrade copyright protection in their own countries.

For example, in 1993, countries of the European Union decided (with heavy involvement by the continent's publishers), as part of efforts to harmonize their various national copyright laws, to extend copyright protection from the life of the author plus 50 years, or 75 years for works owned by corporations (as specified in the Berne Convention), to the life of the author plus 70 years, or 95 years for works owned by corporations. Shortly afterward, U.S. intellectual property associations began lobbying Congress for an identical term of protection arguing–as Fritz Attaway, General Counsel for the Motion Picture Association of America (MPAA), put it in 1997 congressional testimony–that "as the world leader in producing copyrighted works, it would be unseemly, and just plain unthinkable, for the U.S. to lag behind other nations in protecting its copyright industry."[11] Legislation permitting this extension–which would keep copyrighted works out of the public domain for an additional 20 years, at considerable cultural cost to the nation–has passed the House and is currently being considered in the Senate.

If the protection of copyrighted works is to continue to serve the broad public interest, as specified in the U.S. Constitution, librarians, educators, and other representatives of the public interest will have to let Congress and the executive branch know why copyright owners' understandable desires to safeguard and supplement their revenue streams need to be better balanced against the needs of the larger society for a reasonably free flow of information.

NOTES

1. Edward W. Ploman and L. Clark Hamilton, *Copyright: Intellectual Property in the Information Age* (London and Boston: Routledge & Kegan Paul, 1980), p. 1.

2. Ibid., p. 2.

3. Lyman Ray Patterson, *Copyright in Historical Perspective* (Nashville, Tennessee: Vanderbilt University Press, 1968), pp. 6-7.

4. Ithiel de Sola Pool, *Technologies of Freedom* (London and Cambridge, Massachusetts: Belknap Press of Harvard University Press, 1983), pp. 16-17.

5. For further information on electronic rights management systems (ERMSs), see Daniel J. Gervais, "Electronic Rights Management Systems (ERMS): The Next Logical Step in the Evolution of Rights Management," paper presented at a conference held in Seville, Spain in May 1997. It can be found on the World Wide Web, on

the (U.S.) Copyright Clearance Center's site, at *http://www.copyright.com/stuff/ecms_network.htm*. See also Clifford Lynch, "Identifiers and Their Role in Networked Information Applications," in the Association of Research Libraries' *ARL: A Bimonthly Newsletter of Research Library Issues*, No. 194 (October 1997), pp. 12-16.

6. Doreen Carvajal, "Electronic 'Branding' Receives Accolades at the Frankfurt Book Fair," *New York Times*, October 20, 1997, p. D11.

7. For an interesting, though clearly partisan, discussion of the background to, and the actual WIPO Treaty negotiations at, the Geneva conference, see two articles that appeared, under the heading "Confab Clips Copyright Cartel," in the March 1997 issue (Vol. 5, No. 3) of *Wired* magazine: Pamela Samuelson, "Big Media Beaten Back," pp. 61-64+; and John Browning, "Africa 1, Hollywood 0," pp. 61-64+.

8. For further details on the copyright treaty that emerged from the December 1996 Geneva conference, see World Intellectual Property Organization, "Diplomatic Conference on Certain Copyright and Neighboring Rights Questions: Agreed Statements Concerning the WIPO Copyright Treaty," WIPO Document No. CRNR/DC/6 (English), December 23, 1996, available on WIPO's Web site at *http://www.wipo.org/eng/diplconf/distrib/96dc.htm*. See also WIPO Press Release No. 106 (English), (untitled), December 20, 1996, available on WIPO's Web site at *http://www.wipo.org/eng/diplconf/distrib/press106.htm*.

9. World Intellectual Property Organization, "WIPO Copyright Treaty (Geneva, 1996): Status on May 25, 1998," available on WIPO's Web site at *http://www.wipo.org/eng/ratific/s-copy.htm*.

10. World Intellectual Property Organization, Information Meeting on Intellectual Property in Databases, Paragraph 10 (chairman's summary of the discussion) of "Report adopted by the Information Meeting," WIPO Document No. DB/IM/6 (English), page 3, available on WIPO's Web site at *http://www.wipo.org/eng/meetings/infdat97/db_im_6.htm*.

11. As quoted in Gail Russell Chaddock, "When Is Art Free?" *Christian Science Monitor*, June 11, 1998, available on the newspaper's web site at *www.csmonitor.com/durable/1998/06/11/p51s1.htm*.

Copyright and Fair Use
of Multimedia Resources

Norman Desmarais

Only one thing is impossible for God: to find any sense in any copyright law on the planet. Whenever a copyright law is to be made or altered, then the idiots assemble.

–Mark Twain, *Mark Twain's Notebook,* May 23, 1903

Copyright is a relatively recent concept in international law. Paul Revere's engraving of the Boston Massacre has actually become more famous than the work of Henry Pelham which Revere pirated and re-published with impunity in March, 1770. Book piracy also flourished in 18th century America as publishers re-printed pirated editions of British books for American readers. Yet, nobody complained, as the sharing and communication of ideas seemed more important than the ownership of those ideas. Consider the vast quantity of material published by those prolific writers "Anon" and "Anonymous."

It was only when authors and artists saw the support of their wealthy patrons diminish and eventually disappear that they had to rely on the public for their livelihoods. The protection of intellectual property then took on a greater urgency and resulted in the promulgation of copyright legislation. Copyright is based on the principle that,

Norman Desmarais is Acquisitions Librarian, Phillips Memorial Library, Providence College, Providence, RI 02918.

[Haworth co-indexing entry note]: "Copyright and Fair Use of Multimedia Resources." Desmarais, Norman. Co-published simultaneously in *The Acquisitions Librarian* (The Haworth Information Press, an imprint of The Haworth Press, Inc.) No. 26, 2001, pp. 27-59; and: *Publishing and the Law: Current Legal Issues* (ed: A. Bruce Strauch) The Haworth Information Press, an imprint of The Haworth Press, Inc., 2001, pp. 27-59. Single or multiple copies of this article are available for a fee from The Haworth Document Delivery Service [1-800-342-9678, 9:00 a.m. - 5:00 p.m. (EST). E-mail address: getinfo@haworthpressinc.com].

even though it is intangible, information can be owned. The expression of one's ideas in fixed form constitutes property just as much as the fabrication of a tangible object. Copyright, then, attempts to balance an owner's rights and users' rights and tries to regulate the economy that surrounds these rights.

As statutory enactments, copyright laws apply to everybody; but they govern copying principally. Copyright protects only creative expression, not facts or ideas. Copying raw factual information from a telephone directory or a baseball box score is not infringement, no matter how much money the copier makes. (Licensing, a much more recent development in the regulation of intellectual property, is broader in scope as it stipulates how that property can be used.)

In this paper, we plan to review the history and development of copyright in the United States and the formulation of the concept of fair use. We shall look at the principle of fair use and its application in higher education, examining the four factors to keep in mind in deciding whether an application is fair use or not. We shall also examine the development, formulation, and status of the Fair Use Guidelines for Educational Multimedia produced by the Committee on Fair Use.

We shall then consider what is happening on the international front regarding copyright protection and fair use in the digital era. We shall look at the provisions of the treaties emanating from the World Intellectual Property Organization, the ratification process, and U.S. legislative efforts to implement those treaties, particularly the Digital Millennium Copyright Act. We shall also provide some resources for educators to consider in deciding whether or not their applications constitute fair use.

COPYRIGHT AND FAIR-USE BASICS

The first real copyright law dates back to 1710 when the British Parliament forbade the unauthorized printing, reprinting, or importing of books for a limited number of years. The first American copyright law did not emerge until 1790. It was based on Art. I, Sect. 8 of the Constitution of the United States which gives Congress the power "to promote the progress of science and useful arts, by securing for limited times to authors and inventors the exclusive right to their respective writings and discoveries."

But even when Congress broadened U.S. copyright laws in 1897 to include public performances of musical works, those laws were still widely flouted and had to be reworked in 1909. The new law, which passed on March 4 and took effect July 1, 1909, would remain unchanged for 68 years. It would let the courts define the doctrine of "fair use" which would take into account the nature of the copyrighted work, the amount of material copied, and the effect of the use on the copyright owner's potential market when deciding cases involving charges of copyright infringement.

Copyright law begins with the premise that the copyright owner has exclusive rights to many uses of a protected work. The Copyright Act of 1976 (17 USCA §106) identifies five separate rights:

1. The right to reproduce or copy the work;
2. The right to prepare derivative works;
3. The right to distribute copies of the work to the public;
4. The right to perform the work publicly, in the case of audiovisual works;
5. The right to display the work publicly, in the case of literary, musical, dramatic, and choreographic works, pantomimes, and pictorial, graphic, or sculptural works, including the individual images of a motion picture or other audiovisual work.

Justice Sandra Day O'Connor, in the 1991 Feist decision (Feist Publications, Inc. v. Rural Telephone Service Co., 499 US 340, 349), stated that "the primary objective of copyright is not to reward the labor of authors, but 'to promote the Progress of Science and useful Arts'. To this end, copyright assures authors the right to their original expression, but encourages others to build freely upon the ideas and information conveyed by a work . . . This result is neither unfair nor unfortunate. It is the means by which copyright advances the progress of science and art."

The Copyright Act also sets forth several important exceptions to the rights outlined in §106. Key statutes make specific allowance for concerns such as distance learning, backup copies of software, and some reproductions made by libraries. The best known and most important exception to owners' rights is fair use introduced in the Copyright Law of 1909 and expanded by the Copyright Act of 1976.

The following is the full text of the fair-use statute from the U.S. Copyright Act.

Section 107 of the Copyright Act of 1976. Limitations on exclusive rights: Fair use

Notwithstanding the provisions of sections 106 and 106A, the fair use of a copyrighted work, including such use by reproduction in copies or phonorecords or by any other means specified in that section, for purposes such as criticism, comment, news reporting, teaching (including multiple copies for classroom use), scholarship, or research, is not an infringement of copyright. In determining whether the use made of a work in any particular case is a fair use the factors to be considered shall include–

1. the purpose and character of the use, including whether such use is of a commercial nature or is for nonprofit educational purposes;
2. the nature of the copyrighted work;
3. the amount and substantiality of the portion used in relation to the copyrighted work as a whole; and
4. the effect of the use upon the potential market for or value of the copyrighted work.

The fact that a work is unpublished shall not itself bar a finding of fair use if such finding is made upon consideration of all the above factors (17 USCA §107). Section 107 of the U.S. Copyright Act of 1976, which took effect January 1, 1978, embodies the concept of fair use today by exempting limited uses of materials from infringement liabilities. The fair-use statute makes clear that the right of fair use is specifically applicable to teaching, research, and scholarship, and that its scope depends on four factors which are open to different interpretations. However, the law offers virtually no details for determining which activities may be safely allowed.

The genius of United States copyright law is that, in conformance with its constitutional foundation, it balances the intellectual property interests of authors, publishers, and copyright owners with society's need for the free exchange of ideas. Taken together, fair use and other public rights to utilize copyrighted works, as confirmed in the Copyright Act of 1976, constitute indispensable legal doctrines for promoting the dissemination of knowledge, while ensuring authors, publishers, and copyright owners appropriate protection of their creative works and economic investments.

FAIR USE AND HIGHER EDUCATION: A STATEMENT OF PRINCIPLE

The concept of fair use and its application in higher education is based on the idea that the fundamental mission of higher education is to advance and disseminate knowledge. Educators must use a variety of information formats, learning environments, and teaching methods without unreasonable copyright restrictions to fulfill this mission. They must have the ability to explore, analyze, and exchange information freely and to be able to make creative and balanced fair use of copyrighted works to be effective in their work.

Fair use is a historically important doctrine which is essential to fulfilling the objectives of higher education. It allows educators to respond to the dynamic nature of the educational process and to the evolving formats of information resources. Fair use allows an otherwise rigid copyright system to respond to the fluctuating volume of available information and to the changing demands for its use. It permits educators and students to explore a broad range of ideas, to build new works upon the old, and to facilitate equal access to copyrighted works within the reasonable limits of the law.

While educational objectives and activities are noble and laudable, an educational purpose alone does not make a use fair. In fact, the purpose of the use is only one of four factors that users must consider in determining whether or not an activity is a lawful one according to the principles of fair use. While Congress deemed nonprofit educational uses more favorably than commercial uses, the courts may not view the use of copies made or sold at monetary profit and used in education as favorably. Courts are also more apt to favor uses that are "transformative" or that are not mere reproductions. A work which uses a copyrighted work to create something new, such as quotations incorporated into a paper or pieces of a work mixed into a multimedia product for educational purposes, is more likely to be considered an application of fair use.

The nature of the work being used is a second factor to consider. The courts are more likely to favor the fair use of nonfiction rather than fiction, a "permanent" publication rather than a consumable one like a workbook, and the use of printed works over commercial audiovisual works. However, they are still undecided on whether a published work that is currently out of print should receive special treatment.

A third factor involves the amount of material copied, although the law does not specify any exact measures of allowable quantity. Several organizations, particularly those participating in or endorsing the work of the Committee on Fair Use (CONFU), have tried to come to some agreement in formulating guidelines that cover both the quantity and the quality of the material permitted to be copied under fair use. Quantity must be evaluated relative to the length of the entire original and the amount needed to serve a proper objective.

The final factor, which is perhaps even more complicated than the other three, considers the effect on the market. It basically tries to protect the financial interests of the creators and copyright holders. If a derivative product has a negative impact on the sale of the original, such a product would not likely be considered fair use, regardless of one's personal willingness or ability to pay for such purchase.

"Effect" and "purpose" are closely related; so it may be difficult to prove market effect for products with a purpose of research or scholarship. However, for products with a commercial purpose, the effect is presumed. While occasional quotations or photocopies may have little or no adverse market effects, certain reproductions, such as of software, musical recordings, and videotapes, can have a direct impact on the potential markets for those works.

One court has ruled that a journal article alone is an entire work; any copying of an entire work usually weighs heavily against fair use. Pictures generate serious controversies, because a user nearly always wants the full image or the full "amount." Motion pictures are also problematic because even short clips may borrow the most extraordinary or creative elements. One may also reproduce only a small portion of any work but still take "the heart of the work." The "substantiality" concept is a qualitative measure that may weigh against fair use.

FAIR USE GUIDELINES IN AN ELECTRONIC AGE

The educational and research communities believe that the right of fair use must continue unencumbered by terms of licenses or transaction fees in the electronic era. To that end, the Committee on Fair Use (CONFU) was established to discuss intellectual property with the intent of preserving the balance of interests and rights of copyright owners and users in the digital environment. It started with forty members and eventually grew to around a hundred organizations representing for-profit and not-for-profit publishers, the software industry, government agencies, scholars and scholarly societies, authors, artists, photographers and musicians, the movie industry, public television, licensing collectives, libraries, museums, universities and colleges. It also included representatives of a number of library associations, such as the American Library Association, American Association of Law Libraries, Association of Academic Health Sciences Library Directors, Association of Research Libraries, Medical Library Association, and Special Libraries Association, and received the endorsement of the Art Libraries Society of North America.

Believing that the benefits of new technologies should flow to the public as well as to copyright proprietors, the representatives aimed to protect the public's legitimate right to use copyrighted material as more information becomes available only in electronic formats. They also believed that these lawful uses of copyrighted works must be allowed without individual transaction fees. Those discussions resulted in the statement entitled "Fair Use in the Electronic Age: Serving the Public Interest" which aimed to provide guidance on the application of fair-use principles by educators, scholars, and students who develop multimedia projects using portions of copyrighted works under fair use rather than by seeking authorization for non-commercial educational uses.

Aware that only the courts can determine authoritatively whether a particular use is fair use, the consensus of the participants was that the guidelines represent conditions under which fair use should generally apply and provide examples of when permission is required. Uses that exceed these guidelines may or may not be fair use. The participants also agreed that the more one exceeds these guidelines, the greater the risk that fair use does not apply.

The guidelines state that the uses of creative works in the creation of educational multimedia projects are subject to time, portion, copying, and distribution limitations and should include proper attribution and citation.

Time Limitations

Educators may use their educational multimedia projects created for educational purposes for teaching courses, for a period of up to two years after the first instructional use with a class. Use beyond that time period, even for educational purposes, requires permission for each copyrighted portion incorporated in the production.

Portion Limitations

The guidelines try to quantify the amounts of the various types of media that can be used reasonably under the terms of fair use. They use the term "portion limitations" to refer to the amount of a copyrighted work that can be used reasonably in educational multimedia projects regardless of the original medium from which the copyrighted works are taken. The phrase "in the aggregate" refers to the total amount of copyrighted material from a single copyrighted work that is permitted to be used in an educational multimedia project without permission. The portion limitations apply cumulatively to each educator's or student's multimedia project(s) for the same academic semester, cycle, or term.

The guidelines specify the portion limitations for the various types of media as follows:

Text Material. Up to 10% or 1000 words, whichever is less, in the aggregate of a copyrighted work consisting of text material may be reproduced or otherwise incorporated as part of an educational multimedia project. An entire poem of less than 250 words may be used but no more than three poems by one poet or five poems by different poets from any anthology may be used. For poems of greater length, 250 words may be used but no more than three excerpts by a poet or five excerpts by different poets from a single anthology may be used.

Motion Media. Up to 10% or three minutes, whichever is less, in the aggregate of a copyrighted motion media work may be reproduced or otherwise incorporated as part of an educational multimedia project.

Music, Lyrics, and Music Video. Up to 10%, but in no event more than 30 seconds, of the music and lyrics from an individual musical work (or in the aggregate of extracts from an individual work), whether the musical work is embodied in copies or audio or audiovisual works, may be reproduced or otherwise incorporated as a part of a multimedia project. Any alterations to a musical work shall not change the basic melody or the fundamental character of the work.

Illustrations and Photographs. The reproduction or incorporation of photographs and illustrations is more difficult to define with regard to fair use because fair use usually precludes the use of an entire work. Under the guidelines, a photograph or illustration may be used in its entirety but no more than five images by an artist or photographer may be reproduced or otherwise incorporated as part of an educational multimedia project. When using photographs and illustrations from a published collective work, not more than 10% or 15 images, whichever is less, may be reproduced or otherwise incorporated as part of an educational multimedia project.

Numerical Data Sets. Up to 10% or 2500 fields or cell entries, whichever is less, from a copyrighted database or data table may be reproduced or otherwise incorporated as part of an educational multimedia project. A field entry is defined as a specific item of information, such as a name or Social Security number, in a record of a database file. A cell entry is defined as the intersection where a row and a column meet on a spreadsheet.

Copying and Distribution Limitations

The guidelines also specify limits for copying and distribution. They state that "only a limited number of copies, including the original, may be made of an educator's educational multimedia project" and that "there may be no more than two use copies only one of which may be placed on reserve." An additional copy may be made for preservation purposes but may only be used or copied to replace a use copy that has been lost, stolen, or damaged. Also the creators of an educational multimedia project may each make a copy.

Educators and students are advised to note that if there is a possibility that their own educational multimedia project incorporating copyrighted works under fair use could later result in broader dissemination, whether or not as a commercial product, it is strongly recommended that they take steps to obtain permissions during the development process for all copyrighted portions rather than waiting until after completion of the project.

Despite all the two and a half years of discussions that led to the formulation of these guidelines, completed in November, 1996, CONFU participants and representatives from both the copyright owner and user communities who once supported or endorsed the guidelines could not reach a consensus in supporting them. Realizing they could go no further in their deliberations, CONFU members, at their meeting on May 19, 1997, concluded that the working group could not agree on recommending the guidelines for endorsement. They did agree, however, that the draft guidelines could be disseminated to organizations for review, discussion, and possible endorsement.

In some areas, participants felt that the time was not yet ripe to write actual guidelines since the technology was still evolving and the marketplace was still experimenting with how to deal with these issues. Some users thought the guidelines were too restrictive; and copyright owners thought they were giving away too much. In other areas, there was no clear consensus on how to draft guidelines, or whether, in some cases, guidelines were even necessary. Some institutions and organizations which participated in CONFU were opposed to one or more of the proposals for guidelines, while others endorsed some or all of the guidelines.

> Since many CONFU participants voiced support for the guidelines, and the guidelines were already being implemented in several educational institutions around the country, it was decided that the Educational Multimedia Fair Use Guidelines would be released in their present and final form. It was suggested that the implementation of the guidelines be observed over the course of the next year, and it was further agreed that a report on the implementation of the guidelines would be made at a meeting on May 18, 1998. (The Conference on Fair Use: Report to the Commissioner on the Conclusion of the First Phase of the Conference on Fair Use. September, 1997: http://www.uspto.gov/web/offices/dcom/olia/confu/conclutoc.html)

CONFU planned to reconvene on May 18, 1998 to assess the status of the three sets of guidelines (educational multimedia, electronic reserve systems, and copyrighted computer programs in libraries), to take reports on the work of the remaining working groups on digital images and distance learning, and to assess the progress, if any, toward achieving greater acceptance, endorsement, and implementation of the various sets of guidelines within the copyright owner and user communities.

The guidelines for the fair use of educational multimedia took into consideration what the participants considered reasonable interpretations of the Copyright Law and its interpretation in recent court cases, such as Basic Books, Inc. v. Kinko's Graphics Corp., 758 F.Supp. 1522 (S.D.N.Y. 1991); Maxtone-Graham v. Burtchaell, 803 F.2d 1253 (2d Cir. 1986), cert. denied, 481 U.S. 1059 (1987); Encyclopaedia

Britannica Educational Corp. v. Crooks, 542 F.Supp. 1156 (W.D.N.Y. 1982); and American Geophysical Union v. Texaco Inc., 37 F.2d 881 (2d Cir. 1994), modified, 60 F.3d 913 (1995).

While there is no agreement in CONFU on recommending or endorsing the guidelines, it seems reasonable that the closer one sticks to the guidelines the more likely the courts would consider the uses to comply with the principle of fair use. Applications that exceed the guidelines may or may not be fair use; and the more one exceeds the guidelines, the greater the risk that fair use does not apply.

WORLD INTELLECTUAL PROPERTY ORGANIZATION TREATIES

The Committee on Fair Use worked on formulating its guidelines to interpret and apply the U.S. Copyright Act of 1976 for multimedia projects, primarily those in a digital environment. The rest of the world needed to grapple with the same issues at the same time. The World Intellectual Property Organization (WIPO), a United Nations agency since 1974, met in Geneva from December 2-20, 1996. Delegates from 160 nations gathered for the first time in 25 years to update the Berne Convention (1886) on literary and artistic rights and the Rome Convention (1961) on musical rights. The intention was to bring these conventions more into line with the realities of an increasingly networked and electronic world.

WIPO brought three draft treaties to the conference that would deal with: (1) the protection of literary and artistic works, (2) the protection of rights of performers and producers of phonograms, and (3) intellectual property in respect to databases. Many of the provisions in these proposals echoed controversial elements contained in copyright legislation stalled in the U.S. Congress.

The debates over the three weeks of the conference dealt with extraordinarily complex legal and technical issues, the significant financial interests at risk, the diversity of technology and network experience across the world, the concentration of intellectual property creation in the United States and Western Europe, and the challenges of reaching international agreements.

The database treaty had provoked massive opposition from both the public and private sectors in the United States, particularly the Internet access providers and the scientific and research communities. The telephone companies and other firms providing Internet connections, such as America Online, complained that they could be held liable for infringements by their customers, even though the companies may be unaware of the violations. The academics, who feared they would be cut off from the information they thrive on, argued that such a treaty would violate the Supreme Court's "sweat of the brow" doctrine [Feist Publications, Inc. v. Rural Telephone Service Co., Inc., 499 U.S. 340 (1991)] that decided that similar information, such as that in telephone directories, cannot be protected because it consists of unprotected facts and lacks originality and creativity. Academics and scientists also worried that database protection did not recognize fair use.

Commercial enterprises, on the other hand, want to protect their investments in data collection and compilation. They often compile this data at great expense and fear that they will lose control over the distribution of that information in a digital environment. However, the protection could go too far if it tempts or encourages database owners to invoke their property rights and require payment from anyone accessing the database on the Internet.

Confused by the draft database treaty and generally unwilling to confront the issues, the delegates decided to postpone discussion to a future meeting. They concentrated their attention on the Copyright Treaty and the Performances and Phonograms Treaty.

WIPO Copyright Treaty

The preamble of the WIPO Copyright Treaty recognizes "the need to maintain a balance between the interests of the authors and the larger public interest, particularly education, research, and access to information." It thus preserves fair use and other balancing principles of traditional copyright law; but the battle for balance in laws affecting intellectual property rights in the digital environment is far from over.

The treaty provides protection for any original use or reproduction of artistic work. This means that the individual who has the right of distribution under international copyright law–usually the creator of the material–has the right to release or sell artistic works such as graphics, music, and scanned photographs. The treaty accords computer programs the same protection as literary works "regardless of the mode or form of their expression." It also accords protection to "compilations of data or other material, in any form, which by reason of the selection or arrangement of their contents constitute intellectual creations" but does not extend the protection to the data or the material itself.

The treaty essentially preserves the copyright status quo in the U.S. However, negotiators agreed to include two key provisions that will help network managers. First, the delegates eliminated Article 7 which was very important to information professionals, as it tried to extend copyright protection to the temporary copying performed in networks and computers. The article would have required signatories to treat temporary copies, such as those made in random access memory (RAM) as information travels over the Internet, as a "reproduction." This could have violated the exclusive reproduction right. The networked nature of the information infrastructure would require that the most restrictive set of national laws would govern the conduct in the global information infrastructure.

Several nations realized the potentially harmful effects that Article 7 would have had on the global information infrastructure by outlawing the downloading of Web sites in the course of viewing material. The delegates decided that "the mere provision of physical facilities for enabling or making a communication" does not in itself amount to communication. Therefore, a company cannot be sued for copyright infringement just because it provides the physical facilities, such as a computer network, used in the violation. They also decided that a temporary copy should not be considered a true copy for copyright purposes. The provision was consequently dropped from Article 7.

WIPO Performances and Phonograms Treaty

The final treaty, the WIPO Performances and Phonograms Treaty, gives authors the right to control digital transmissions of their works insofar as these constitute a communication of their works to the public.

The key elements of the treaty include:

- Moral and economic rights of performers are specified along with rights of reproduction, distribution, and rental.
- Record companies have more control over on-demand services, such as music delivered electronically; but there's still more work to do in this area.
- Limitations and exceptions to use of services have been strengthened. Broad exemption of "personal use" has been nar-

rowed to prevent "personal use" of material if that infringes on copyright.
* New language prohibits circumvention of copyright devices.

Jason Berman, Chairman of the Recording Industry Association of America (RIAA), said that none of changes agreed to at the WIPO conference require changes in U.S. copyright law. He also stated that the record industry has a $40-billion global market, $12.3 billion of that in the U.S. The U.S. share of the world market has dropped to about 30%, down from more than 40% 10 years ago, even as the market has grown in the last decade. If the industry wants to expand overseas, he said, it will need strong protection that the WIPO treaty provides.

For an overview of the WIPO home page, the proposed treaties, and the treaties as adopted, see *http://www.wipo.org/eng/iplex/index.htm; http://www.wipo.org/eng/diplconf/distrib/89dc.htm*; and *http://www.wipo.org/eng/diplconf/distrib/95dc.htm*

Ratification

While the delegates of the 160 member nations endorsed the two WIPO treaties, their respective governments must work out many of the details and ratify them within two years. The treaties will become effective worldwide when the 30th signatory nation completes its act of ratification. The signatory nations include eight European Union states, with the remaining seven EU nations committed to joining. As of September 20, 1997, only Indonesia had completed the ratification process.

The ratification process requires much greater political will than does the initial signing. The signature of a nation's head of state commits the country to the documents in principle. But ratification requires the country's legislative body to find both the time and the political support to pass the treaties' provisions into domestic legislation. For the treaty to become binding in the U.S., it then must be ratified by two-thirds of the Senate.

In the Northern Hemisphere, Eastern European governments have made the least progress on passing the WIPO treaties. This is probably because these countries are still coping with the economic legacy of their communist pasts and have not given a high priority so far to granting the advanced level of copyright protection the treaties represent.

U.S. LEGISLATIVE EFFORTS

Both houses of Congress considered more detailed legislation to implement the WIPO treaties in the spring and summer of 1998. Lobbyists pushed for changes in the way the U.S. interprets and implements the treaties–changes that could make it easier to sue companies for infringement if end users send copyrighted works over their networks.

U.S. legislation in 1996 nearly mirrored recommendations made in September, 1995 by the Working Group on Intellectual Property Rights chaired by Bruce A. Lehman, Commissioner of Patents and Trademarks. The group's report, entitled "Intellectual Property and the National Information Infrastructure" (popularly called the White Paper), suggested what initially seemed to be minor adjustments to current law. However, the issues under discussion at WIPO in Geneva were much broader.

U.S. legislation included:

- The coverage of electronically transmitted works under the protection of copyright. This would protect a work whenever a copy of it "is fixed beyond the place from which it was sent." The WIPO treaty would also protect those works, except for those stored temporarily in computer equipment before transmission over the Internet.
- A criminal ban on importing or manufacturing devices whose main purpose is to bypass or defeat mechanisms that prevent or limit copying of protected works, primarily aimed at those available in a digital versatile disc (DVD) format. The Geneva treaties propose a similar ban but leave the specifics to individual governments.
- In response to the LaMacchia case, replacement of the deliberate commercial exploitation requirement for criminal prosecution with language that would make it a crime to "willfully" distribute copies of works valued at $5,000 or more, regardless of whether the infringer tries to make a profit. [David LaMacchia, a student at MIT, was charged with running an electronic bulletin

board that others used to upload and download illegally more than $1 million in copyrighted software. U.S. District Court Judge Richard Stearns ruled that the old federal wire fraud law under which LaMacchia was indicted was not applicable in his case and suggested Congress plug the holes in laws intended for a pre-cyberspace era. United States v. LaMacchia, 871 F.Supp. 535 (D. Mass. 1994)]

Sen. John Ashcroft (R-MO) introduced the "Digital Copyright Clarification and Technology Act" (S. 1146) in the Senate on September 3, 1997; and Representatives Rick Boucher (D-VA) and Tom Campbell (R-CA) introduced the "Digital Era Copyright Enhancement Act" (H.R 3048) on November 13, 1997, just hours before the First Session of the 105th Congress adjourned.

The purposes of S. 1146 were:

1. to clarify the application of copyright law in the unique environment of Internet and on-line communication;
2. to foster the continued growth and development of the Internet as a means of communication and commerce, including the lawful distribution of intellectual property;
3. to protect the rights of copyright owners in the digital environment;
4. to clarify that providing network services and facilities with respect to the transmission of electronic communications of another person does not result in liability under the Copyright Act;
5. to clarify that Internet and on-line service providers are not liable for third-party copyright infringements unless they have received notice in compliance with this Act of the infringing material and have a reasonable opportunity to limit the third-party infringement; and
6. to create incentives for the rapid elimination of infringing material residing on an electronic communications system or network without litigation.

The bill also amended Section 117 of title 17, United States Code (Limitations on exclusive rights) by inserting the following as a new subsection (b) to cover computer programs and digital copies:

b. Notwithstanding the provisions of section 106, it is not an infringement to make a copy of a work in a digital format if such copying–
   1. is incidental to the operation of a device in the course of the use of a work otherwise lawful under this title; and
   2. does not conflict with the normal exploitation of the work and does not unreasonably prejudice the legitimate interests of the author.

S. 1146 provides a positive alternative to previous legislation (H.R. 2281 and S. 1121) introduced in response to the adoption of the WIPO treaties but strongly opposed by the American Library Association (ALA) and the Home Recording Rights Coalition (HRRC). The HRRC objected to the part of the bill that would ban the sale of devices or components "primarily designed" to circumvent technological copyright protection. This provision would mean that the courts would have a role in designing new consumer electronics devices. Gary Shapiro, President of HRRC, said Congress "has been asked to deny consumers new models of VCRs, audio recorders, and computers unless they conform to any and all technological anti-copy schemes, both analog and digital, through a provision that may impede technological progress, cause devices to malfunction, and negate the right of consumer fair use." Equipment manufacturers say that the law should outlaw behavior, not devices that may have both infringing and non-infringing uses.

The Digital Era Copyright Enhancement Act (H.R 3048) would have amended current copyright law to:

• Extend the Fair Use Doctrine to apply in the digital environment.
• Allow libraries and archives to use the latest technology to preserve and store endangered material without fear of copyright violation.
• Permit educators engaged in distance learning to use computer networks to distribute remotely an appropriate variety of materials directly related to a defined curriculum to students enrolled in their classes.
• Disallow the consideration of electronic copies of material incidentally or temporarily made in the process of using a computer network as the sole basis for copyright infringement liability.

- Establish liability for individuals who deliberately use a computer network to violate copyright laws, such as circumventing copyright protection systems (passwords, encryption codes). These individuals should be subject to substantial civil (but not criminal) liability.
- Prevent non-negotiated, take-it-or-leave-it licenses like those often found shrink-wrapped with computer software or in on-line transactions from overriding federal copyright law, including rights and privileges that afford access to information.

Barbara J. Ford, ALA President, said that "Representatives Boucher and Campbell have introduced exactly the type of balanced and visionary copyright legislation that our nation needs to ensure that everyone benefits from the Internet's tremendous promise. This excellent bill balances the needs of information proprietors with those of information consumers like teachers, students, software designers, and library users everywhere. It is that balance that has made the U.S. the technological and economic leader that it is and must remain."

The Digital Future Coalition (*http://www.dfc.org*), a group of 39 nonprofit educational, scholarly, library, and consumer groups (including ALA) and major commercial trade associations in the consumer electronics, telecommunications, computer, and network access industries, also endorsed the legislation. However, copyright owners, like the Association of American Publishers (AAP) and the RIAA, supported H.R. 2281 which was drafted more narrowly, focusing on a "device" as a trigger for violations. The new bill (H.R. 3048) contains a circumvention provision in which violations would be triggered by illegal "conduct" rather than by use of a "device."

RIAA officials, singer/songwriter Johnny Cash, and songwriters representing ASCAP and BMI appeared before the House Intellectual Property Subcommittee on the WIPO Copyright Treaties Implementation Act (H.R. 2180) and the On-Line Copyright Liability Limitation Act (H.R. 2281) over two days of hearings September 16 and 17, 1997 to push for quick ratification of the treaty.

Some members of Congress and the copyright industries, which include U.S. record and movie companies, were concerned that ratification of the treaties would be impeded. These company leaders feared that the objections of a group of computer and electronic device manufacturers and others who opposed the language of the provision might hamper or unfairly target their products. The opponents were concerned that customers might be victimized by the device language if they used a machine designed primarily for non-infringing uses in a manner that infringed the agreement. They prefered that violations result from the conduct in the illegal use rather than from the device used.

The Boucher-Campbell bill changed the language to refer to conduct rather than devices to try to achieve a more "balanced" approach between owners and users. The bill also spelled out an "ephemeral copying" provision that made it explicit that a person who makes a digital copy of a copyrighted work "when such copying is made incidental to the operation of a computer in the course of the use of the work in a way that is otherwise lawful" does not infringe on the copyright.

The Boucher-Campbell bill also stated that the 1976 copyright law's fair-use provisions for scholars and educators should "apply in full force in the digital networked environment." While the bill stated that the copyright law's first-sale provision should allow "electronic transmission of a lawfully acquired digital copy of a work as long as it is erased or destroyed" when an electronic transfer is made by the user, it did not contain any enforcement language.

The Digital Millennium Copyright Act

Although the Bill Clinton/Monica Lewinski affair and Congressional bickering delayed consideration of copyright legislation, Congress finally got around to debating some 30 bills to modify the copyright law, many in multiple versions. Before adjourning, the 105th Congress passed two major pieces of copyright legislation: the Sonny Bono Copyright Term Extension Act and the Digital Millennium Copyright Act of 1998 (DMCA). President Clinton signed the former into law on October 27 and the latter the following day. Congress tabled the database protection bill just as the WIPO delegates did, leaving the 106th Congress to revive it.

The Sonny Bono Copyright Term Extension Act (PL 105-928) extends the duration of a copyright by twenty years for works published after January 1, 1978. The copyright for works by a single author now lasts for the life of the author plus seventy years (formerly life plus fifty). The copyright for works of joint authorship endures for the life of the last surviving author plus seventy years. Anonymous and pseudonymous works and works made for hire have a copyright period that extends for ninety-five years (formerly seventy-five years) from the date of first publication or 120 years from the date of first creation.

To offset the impact that this extension may have on libraries, the Act also amends 17 USC § 108 to allow a library, archives, or a nonprofit educational institution that functions as such to "reproduce, distribute, display, or perform in facsimile or digital form a copy or phonorecord of such work, or portions thereof, for purposes of preservation, scholarship, or research" under certain specified conditions during the last twenty years of any term of copyright of a published work. In essence, this allows libraries and archives to treat this material as if it were in the public domain during this period. The law goes on to state, however, that the exemption does not extend "to any subsequent uses by users other than such library or archives," apparently excluding use by library patrons.

The DMCA is based on The On-Line Copyright Liability Limitation Act (H.R. 2281) which was modified to include provisions from many pieces of alternative legislation such as Sen. John Ashcroft's "Digital Copyright Clarification and Technology Act" (S. 1146) and Rep. Rick Boucher's and Rep. Tom Campbell's "Digital Era Copyright Enhancement Act" (HR 3048).

Title I of the DMCA, called the WIPO Copyright and Performances and Phonograms Treaties Implementation Act of 1998, amends Title 17 of the United States Code to comply with the WIPO Copyright Treaty and the WIPO Performances and Phonograms Treaty. It also adds a new chapter, Chapter 12 (Circumvention of Copyright Protection Systems), to comply with the provisions in the WIPO treaties that require contracting parties to provide legal remedies against circumventing technological protection measures and tampering with copyright management information. The law sets up a process for individuals to appeal to the Librarian of Congress for an exemption during the three-year period following passage of the DMCA if they believe that they are adversely affected by the prohibitions or if they no longer have access to materials they did under the traditional fair-use provisions of the copyright law.

The DMCA makes hacking illegal by prohibiting circumvention of technological protection measures that control access to a copyrighted work. It also prohibits manufacturing, distributing, or making available technologies, products, and services to defeat or circumvent these controls, such as measures which prevent reproduction. But, to ensure that legitimate multipurpose devices can continue to be produced and sold, the prohibition applies only to those devices that:

1. are primarily designed or produced for the purpose of circumventing;
2. have only a limited commercially significant purpose or use other than to circumvent; or
3. are marketed for use in circumventing.

The DMCA preserves the rights of fair use and grants exemptions for nonprofit libraries, archives, and educational institutions. It protects activities such as computer security testing, reverse engineering to achieve interoperability, the preservation of materials by libraries and archives, the protection of personal privacy, and parental supervision of minors on the Internet. The DMCA permits the manufacture of components to assist parents in preventing minors from accessing pornography and other harmful material on the Internet, provided that the product containing such components does not itself violate the provisions of Title I.

The DMCA creates both civil and criminal penalties for violating Sections 1201 or 1202 by giving the courts broad powers to grant injunctions and award damages, costs, and attorney's fees. The court may also order the impounding, the remedial modification, or the destruction of the devices or products involved in the violation. The court may decide to reduce damage awards against innocent violators or punish repeat offenders by awarding treble damage awards. But, in the case of nonprofit libraries, archives, or educational institutions, the court must remit damages if it finds that the institution had no reason to know of the violation. Willful violations committed for commercial advantage or private financial gain are subject to significant criminal penalties; but nonprofit libraries, archives, and educational institutions are exempt from these criminal penalties.

Title I also makes it illegal to remove or alter the copyright management information accompanying a copyrighted work. It contains a variety of technical amendments granting copyright protection to: (1) sound recordings that were first fixed in a treaty party (a country or intergovernmental organization other than the United States that is a party to specified international copyright and other agreements); and (2) pictorial, graphic, or sculptural works incorporated in a building or other structure or an architectural work embodied in a building located in the United States or a treaty party. The DMCA treats works published in the United States or a treaty party within 30 days after publication in a non-U.S., non-treaty party as first published in the United States or a treaty party for purposes of conferring protection.

Title II of the DMCA limits the liability an on-line service provider (OSP) might incur for copyright infringement. The Act defines "service provider" very broadly in some instances so that many entities which do not provide on-line services as a business may still take advantage of the protection afforded by Title II. One could construe this section to mean that librarians who allow users to access computers and computer networks in their facilities are also OSPs and enjoy the protections of Title II. These protections are in addition to those that an OSP might have under copyright law or any other law.

The Act covers two specific activities: (1) the "intermediate and temporary storage of material on a system or network controlled or operated by or for the service provider," such as system caching or the temporary storage of a Web page or chat room and (2) referring or linking users to infringing material or activity at other on-line locations via a "directory, index, reference pointer or hypertext link." This includes the use of a search engine or a list of recommended sites, for example. The Act also protects an OSP when it acts as a conduit for material traveling between other parties or when a user stores material "on a system or network controlled or operated by or for the service provider" without his or her knowledge.

The DMCA limits the liability of nonprofit educational institutions when its employees use copyrighted material for teaching and research. However, individuals may remain liable for misuse of these materials.

Title III amends Section 117 of the Copyright Act to protect independent service organizations when they make a copy in the maintenance or repair of a computer. This resulted from the case of MAI Systems Corp. vs. Peak Computer, Inc. [991 F.2d 511 (9th Cir. 1993)]. Section 117 of 17 U.S.C. allows the "owner" of a program to load the program into the machine's random access memory (RAM). However, although MAI's client had a license to use the software, it did not own the software. The court decided that MAI infringed the copyright by loading the software into the RAM of the client's computer, thereby making a "reproduction" of the copy. Title III overrules the MAI decision by allowing the owner or licensee of a machine to make or authorize the making of a copy of a computer program under certain conditions when repairing or maintaining the computer hardware.

The Act allows making a copy (1) if the copy is made "solely by virtue of the activation of a machine that lawfully contains an authorized copy of the computer program, for purposes only of maintaining or repairing that machine," (2) if the new copy is used for no other purpose and is destroyed upon completion of the maintenance or repair, and (3) if "any computer program . . . that is not necessary for that machine to be activated . . . is not accessed or used other than to make such new copy by virtue of the activation of the machine." The exception applies only to RAM copies made during the course of hardware maintenance, not software maintenance.

Title IV covers miscellaneous provisions such as the making of ephemeral recordings, recommendations on how to promote distance education through digital technologies, and exemptions for libraries and archives.

The DMCA addresses two issues regarding ephemeral recordings in the digital age. First is the relationship between the ephemeral recording exemption and the Digital Performance Right in Sound Recordings Act of 1995 (DPRSRA). Section 402 modifies the language of the ephemeral recording exemption to allow broadcasters to treat digital broadcasts in the same way they do analog broadcasts. The second issue deals with the relationship between the ephemeral recording exemption and section 1201 of the DMCA that deals with tampering with copyright protection measures. Section 402 allows transmitting organizations, under certain limited circumstances, to perform activities that otherwise would violate section 1201(a)(1) of the DMCA when assembling transmission programs and making ephemeral recordings.

Section 403 of the DMCA directs the Register of Copyright to consult with representatives of copyright owners, nonprofit educational institutions, and nonprofit libraries and archives and to submit to the Congress, within six months, recommendations on how to promote distance education through digital technologies.

Section 404 updates section 108 of the Copyright Act to allow libraries and archives to use digital technologies for specified preservation activities. It alleviates the burden of including a copyright notice on reproductions by requiring a copyright notice only when the copy that is reproduced by the library or archive itself bears a notice. It also allows making up to three copies or phonorecords, rather than just one, for purposes of preservation and security. It also permits making copies or phonorecords in both digital and analog formats. However, the digital copies must be used within the library or archives.

IN THE MEANTIME

The DMCA does not seem to resolve many of the issues of fair use of multimedia materials. The 106th Congress may resume discussions of copyright matters tabled by the 105th Congress. While legislators wrestle with formulating fair and equitable laws, educators have several resources to rely on. First of all, the Copyright Clearance Center (CCC), a not-for-profit organization created in 1978 at the suggestion of Congress to facilitate compliance with United States copyright law, provides a central mechanism for users and rights owners to exchange permissions and royalties for textual material. The CCC has collective licensing programs that provide authorized users with a lawful means for making photocopies from its repertoire of more than 1.75 million titles.

The American Society of Composers, Authors, and Publishers (AS-CAP), founded in New York in 1914, and Broadcast Music, Inc. (BMI) are the primary performance rights clearinghouses in the United States for music. ASCAP was founded to protect the interests of music writers, lyricists, and publishers. It will defend its members against illegal public performances for profit of copyrighted musical compositions, will protect them against other forms of infringement, and will collect license fees for authorized performances. BMI, founded by U.S. radio networks to build "an alternate source of music suitable for broadcasting," competes with the ASCAP. It also collects royalties for its members.

Educators have the CONFU guidelines to assist them in interpreting what fair use means for them. In addition, a group of George Washington University graduate students also developed a web site to help provide guidance. Entitled Copyright Bay, this site (*http://www.wtaccess. com/users/gummess/coprbay/coprbay.htm*) uses coastal metaphors to help students, teachers, and researchers determine what they can safely copy or use. The "Fair Use Harbor" provides the guidelines for using material safely. "Dist-Ed Point," an area that focuses on distance learning, lies on the eastern end of the harbor, just shy of "Infringement Reef."

Copyright and Multimedia Law for Webbuilders and Multimedia Authors (*http://www.lib.uiowa.edu/proj/webbuilder/copyright.html*), based at the University of Iowa, is an index to on-line materials about copyright. It offers a Crash Course in Copyright that includes summaries of legal opinions that may prove useful to anyone in higher education. It also connects visitors to everything from the United States Copyright Office's web page to a page listing "10 Big Myths About Copyright."

A site maintained by the University of Texas at Austin and Britain's University of Reading (*http://www.lib.utexas.edu/Libs/HRC/WATCH/*) posts information on how to find the copyright holders for thousands of works of art and writings. This could probably offer the best way to avoid legal clashes. Stanford University's Copyright & Fair Use Web Site can help educators keep up with current legislation that may affect intellectual-property issues.

CONCLUSION

We have reviewed the history and development of copyright in the United States and the formulation of the concept of fair use. We looked at the principle of fair use and its application in higher education, examining the four factors to keep in mind in deciding whether an application is fair use or not. We examined the development, formulation, and status of the Fair Use Guidelines for Educational Multimedia produced by the Committee on Fair Use.

We also considered what is happening on the international front regarding copyright protection and fair use in the digital era. We looked at the provisions of the treaties emanating from the World Intellectual Property Organization, the ratification process and U.S. legislative efforts to implement those treaties.

Some observers may construe legislative efforts as targeting the Internet primarily. However, while the popularity and ubiquity of the Internet may prompt consideration of some of the legislation, very few, if any, of the bills are written so narrowly as to focus only on the Internet rather than addressing the broader issues of the digital environment. Efforts to achieve a balance between intellectual property rights and fair use will likely extend into the beginning of the next millennium.

BIBLIOGRAPHY

AAU. Report of the AAU Task Force on Intellectual Property Rights in an Electronic Environment. Submitted to the AAU Presidents Steering Committee. April 4, 1994. Washington, DC. http://www.nlc-bnc.ca/ifla/documents/infopol/copyright/acis.txy

Allen, Charles, M.; Boelzner, David, E. An Overview of Multimedia and the Law. *Journal of Instruction Delivery Systems*. 10:1 (Winter 1996) p28-31.

American Committee for Interoperable Systems, Intellectual Property and the National Information Infrastructure. September 1, 1994. http://www.nlc-bnc.ca/ifla/documents/ infopol/copyright/acis.txt

American Library Association et al. Fair Use in the Electronic Age: Serving the Public Interest. http://www.nlc-bnc.ca/ifla/documents/infopol/copyright/fairuse.txt

Arnett, Nick. The Internet and the Anti-net. http://www.nlc-bnc.ca/ifla/documents/ infopol/copyright/antinet.htm

Association of Research Libraries. Intellectual Property: An ARL Statement of Principles. Adopted by the ARL Membership, May 1994. http://www.nlc-bnc.ca/ifla/documents/infopol/copyright/arl-ip.txt

Barlow, John Perry. The Economy of Ideas–A Framework for Rethinking Patents and Copyrights in the Digital Age (Everything you know about intellectual property is wrong). *Wired* Issue 2.03–March 1994. http://www.hotwired.com/wired/2.03/features/economy.ideas.html

Bellingham, Katy and Lavrencic, Tamara. Copyright Impediments to the Preservation of Australia's Documentary Heritage. *Australian Library Review* 12: 4 (November 1995) http://www.nlc-bnc.ca/ifla/documents/infopol/copyright/kbel11.htm

Berry, John W. Statement on Behalf of the University Library, The University of Illinois at Chicago. Working Group on Intellectual Property of the Information Policy Committee of the National Information Infrastructure Task Force. September 22, 1994. http://www.nlc-bnc.ca/ifla/documents/infopol/copyright/berj1.txt

Blumenstyk, Goldie. Educators and Publishers Reach Agreement on "Fair Use" Guidelines for CD-ROMs. *Chronicle-of-Higher-Education*. 43:9 (Oct 25 1996) pA28.

Breslow, Jordan J. Copyright Law. February, 1986. gopher://sulaw.law.su.OZ.AU:70/00/Law Documents/Collection of Various Laws (mainly from U.S.)/copyright.law

Brinson, J. Dianne; Radcliffe, Mark F. Intellectual Property Law Primer for Multimedia Developers. *Community College Journal*. 66:2 (Oct-Nov 1995) p14-18 http://www.timestream.com/web/info/mmlaw.html

British Copyright Council. Oral Response to the National Information Infrastructure Task Force on Intellectual Property. 22nd September 1994. http://www.nlc-bnc.ca/ifla/documents/infopol/copyright/bcc.txt

Bruce, Tom. "Legal Information, Open Models and the Information Highway." Centre de recherche en droit public (CRDP). Crown copyright in Cyberspace. Montréal vendredi, 12 mai 1995. http://www.droit.umontreal.ca/CRDP/Conferences/DAC/BRUCE/BRUCE.html

Bruwelheide, Janis H. *The Copyright Primer for Librarians and Educators*. Second Edition. Chicago: American Library Association, Washington, DC: National Education Association, 1995.

Bruwelheide, Janis H. *Copyright Issues for the Electronic Age*. Syracuse, NY. Washington, DC: ERIC Clearinghouse on Information and Technology, Office of Educational Research and Improvement, 1995.

Burk, Dan L. Trademarks Along the Infobahn: A Look at the Emerging Law of Cybermarks. *Richmond Journal of Law and Technology* 1, April 10, 1995. http://www.urich.edu/~jolt/v1i1/burk.html

Burk, Dan L. Transborder Intellectual Property Issues on the Electronic Frontier. *Stanford Law and Policy Review*. Vol. 5, 1994.

Carroll, Terry. Copyright FAQ. http://www.aimnet.com/~carroll/copyright/faq-home.html

Chase, Mark E. Educators' Attitudes and Related Copyright Issues in Education: A Review of Selected Research 1980-1992. http://www.nlc-bnc.ca/ifla/documents/infopol/copyright/cham.txt

Coalition for Networked Information. "R E A D I (Rights for Electronic Access to and Delivery of Information)." Draft. Negotiating Networked Information Contracts and Licenses. Prepared for CNI by: Robert Ubell and Mark Tesoriero, Robert Ubell Associates, November 15, 1994. http://www.cni.org/projects/READI/guide/www/READI-guide.html

Coalition for Networked Information et al. "Proceedings: Technological Strategies for Protecting Intellectual Property in the Networked Multimedia Environment."

Coalition for Networked Information, Interactive Multimedia Association, John F. Kennedy School of Government, Science, Technology and Public Policy Program, Massachusetts Institute of Technology, Summer 1994. gopher://gopher.cni.org/11/cniftp/miscdocs/ima.ip-workshop

Consortium for Educational Technology for University Systems. Fair Use of Copyrighted Works. http://www.cetus.org/fairindex.html

Coyle, Karen. Copyright in the Digital Age. http://www.dla.ucop.edu/~kec/sfpltalk.html

Crews, Kenneth D. Copyright Law, Libraries, and Universities: Overview, Recent Developments, and Future Issues. Working paper prepared for Association of Research Libraries. October 1992. http://www.nlc-bnc.ca/ifla/documents/infopol/copyright/rights.txt

Crews, Kenneth D. Copyright Law and the Doctoral Dissertation: Guidelines to Your Legal Rights and Responsibilities. n.d. gopher://arl.cni.org:70/00/scomm/copyright/other/crews

Dalziel, Chris. Copyright, Fair Use, and the Information Superhighway. *Community College Journal*. 67:1 (Aug-Sep 1996). p23-27.

Decker, Jack. Christians and the Copyright Law. 1995. http://www.novagate.com/~jack/copyright.html

Demac, Donna. "Property Rights in the Electronic Dawn." REFLEX. August/September 1994. http://www.nlc-bnc.ca/ifla/documents/infopol/copyright/demac2.htm

Demarest, Marc. Controlling Dissemination Mechanisms: The Unstamped Press and the Net. n.d. http://www.nlc-bnc.ca/ifla/documents/infopol/copyright/demm1.htm

Dyson, Esther. Intellectual Value. Wired. Issue 3.07 (July, 1995). http://www.hotwired.com/wired/3.07/features/dyson.html

Ebersole, Joseph L. Response to Dr. Linn's paper "Copyright and Information Services in the Context of the National Research and Education Network." n.d. http://www.nlc-bnc.ca/ifla/documents/infopol/copyright/ebersole.txt

Elias, Steve. Copyrights in Cyberspace. Nolo Press, 1994. http://www.nolo.com/NN197.HTML

Ennis, Willie; Ennis, Demetria. Ten Tips to Aid Teachers Creating Multimedia Presentations. Journal of Computing in Teacher Education. 13:1 (Oct 1996) p16-20.

Erickson, John S. "A Copyright Management System for Networked Interactive Multimedia." Proceedings of the Dartmouth Institute for Advanced Graduate Studies (DAGS). June 1995. http://picard.dartmouth.edu/~oly/DAGS95.html

Erickson, John S. "Can Fair Use Survive Our Information-Based Future?" An IML Technical Report. Spring 1995. http://picard.dartmouth.edu/FairUseInfoFuture. html

Fair Use Guidelines for Educational Multimedia. Liberal Education. 83:1 (Winter 1997) p50-56.

Fernandez, Dennis. Understanding Intellectual Property Rights. 1994. http://www.batnet.com/oikoumene/dfIPRights.html

Field, Thomas G., Jr. "Copyright for Computer Authors." Franklin Pierce Law Center. 1995. http://www.fplc.edu/TFIELD/CopySof.htm

Field, Thomas G., Jr. "Copyright in Visual Arts." Franklin Pierce Law Center. 1995. http://www.fplc.edu/TFIELD/CopyVis.htm

Field, Thomas G., Jr. "Intellectual Property: The Practical and Legal Fundamentals." Franklin Pierce Law Center. 1995. http://www.fplc.edu/tfield/plfip.htm

Fisher, Janet. "Copyright: The Glue of the System." Journal of Electronic Publishing. 1993. http://www.press.umich.edu/jep/works/fisher.copyright.html

Garfinkel, Simson L. Patently Absurd. Wired. July, 1994. http://www.hotwired.com/wired/2.07/features/patents.html

Gassaway, Laura. "When Works Pass Into the Public Domain." 1995. http://smartbiz.com/sbs/arts/ipi5.htm

Gerovac, Branko and Solomon, Richard J. Protect Revenues, Not Bits: Identify Your Intellectual Property. n.d. http://www.nlc-bnc.ca/ifla/documents/infopol/copyright/gerovac.txt

Gloster, Deam M. and McCabe, Kat. Making the New Media Deal. Intellectual Property Magazine. July, 1995. http://www.nlc-bnc.ca/ifla/documents/infopol/copyright/glod1.htm

Graham, Peter S. Intellectual Preservation and Electronic Intellectual Property. n.d. http://www.nlc-bnc.ca/ifla/documents/infopol/copyright/graham.txt

Greguras, Fred, Egger, Michael R. and Wong, Sandy J. Multimedia Content and the Super Highway: Rapid Acceleration or Foot on the Brake? June 18, 1994. http://www.batnet.com/oikoumene/mmcopyright.html

Griswold, Gary N. A Method for Protecting Copyright on Networks. http://www.nlc-bnc.ca/ifla/documents/infopol/copyright/griswold.txt

Halbert, Debora. Computer Technology and Legal Discourse: The Potential for Modern Communication Technology to Challenge Legal Discourses of Authorship and Property. gopher://portia.murdoch.edu.au:70/00/.ftp/pub/subj/law/jnl/elaw/comment/ halbert.txt

Halbert, Martin. Copyright, Digital Media, and Libraries. Recursive Reviews. *The Public-Access Computer Systems Review* 2:1 (1991). p.164-170. gopher://sulaw.law.su.OZ.AU:70/00/Law Documents/Collection of Various Laws (mainly from U.S.)/copyright.libraries

Hardy, Trotter. Contracts, Copyright, and Preemption in a Digital World. *Richmond Journal of Law and Technology.* April 17, 1995. http://www.urich.edu/~jolt/v1i1/hardy.html

Harper, Georgia. Copyright and the University Community. The Office of General Counsel. The University of Texas System. August, 1993. http://www.nlc-bnc.ca/ifla/documents/infopol/copyright/texascp.txt

Holcomb, Terry; Mortensen, Mark. From Atoms to Bits: Suggested Readings on the Road from Traditional to Digital Copyright. *TechTrends.* 42:3 (Apr-May 1997) p10-12.

Index Stock Photography, Inc. "Understanding Copyright Law." http://www.indexstock.com/pages/copyrite.htm

Information Technology Association of Canada. A Copy Is a Copy: Copyright Issues and the Emerging Information Infrastructure. February, 1995. http://www.nlc-bnc.ca/ifla/documents/infopol/copyright/copy95en.htm

Interactive Multimedia Association. Testimony at the public hearing on "Intellectual Property and the National Information Infrastructure." Presented by Brian Kahin. September 22, 1994. http://www.nlc-bnc.ca/ifla/documents/infopol/copyright/ima.txt

International Federation of Library Associations and Institutions (IFLA). Position Paper on Copyright in the Electronic Environment. October 1996. http://www.nlc-bnc.ca/ifla/V/ebpb/copy.htm

International Publishers Association. Position Paper on Libraries, Copyright and the Electronic Environment of the International Publishers Copyright Council (IPCC). 22 April 1996. http://www.nlc-bnc.ca/ifla/documents/infopol/copyright/ipa.txt

Jensen, Michael. Need-Based Intellectual Property Protection and Networked University Press Publishing. http://www.nlc-bnc.ca/ifla/documents/infopol/copyright/jensen.txt

Kahin, Brian. The Strategic Environment for Protecting Multimedia. n.d. http://www.nlc-bnc.ca/ifla/documents/infopol/copyright/kahin.txt

Kahn, Robert E. Deposit, Registration and Recordation in an Electronic Copyright Mangement System. n.d. http://www.nlc-bnc.ca/ifla/documents/infopol/copyright/kahn.txt

Kotlas, Carolyn. Computers and Copyrights: Bibliography. Institute for Academic Technology (IRG-04). http://www.iat.unc.edu/guides/irg-04.html

Lanham, Richard A. *A New Operating System for the Humanities.* Los Angeles: Dept. of English, UCLA, 1994. http://www.nlc-bnc.ca/ifla/documents/infopol/copyright/lanham1.htm

Leaffer, Marshall A. *International Treaties on Intellectual Property,* Second Edition. Edison, NJ: BNA Books, 1997. Softcover/ISBN 1-57018-056-3.

Lehman, Bruce A. Business and Artists' Rights in the Digital Age. Joint Australian/ OECD Conference on Security, Privacy and Intellectual Property Protection in the Global Information Infrastructure. Canberra, 7-8 February 1996. http://www.nla.gov.au/ gii/lehman.html

Lemley, Mark. Rights of Attribution and Integrity in Online Communication. *Journal of Online Law*. June, 1995. http://www.law.cornell.edu/jol/lemley.html

Leventhal, Michael. Who Can Stake a Claim in Cyberspace? http://www.primenet.com/ wiredlaw/domain.htm

Linn, R. J. "Copyright and Information Services in the Context of the National Research and Education Network." NIST. 1993. http://www.hpcc.gov/reports/reports-agencies/ linn.html

Littman, Jessica. "Revising Copyright Law for the Information Age." Twenty-third Annual Telecommunications Policy Research Conference, October 2, 1995. http://swissnet.ai.mit.edu/6805/articles/int-prop/litman-revising/revising.html

Losey, Ralph. "Practical and Legal Protection of Computer Databases." http://seamless. com/rcl/article.html

Loundy, David. "E-Law 3.0: Computer Information Systems Law and System Operator Liability in 1995." http://www.leepfrog.com/E-Law/

Loundy, David. Revising the Copyright Law for Electronic Publishing. *John Marshall Journal of Computer and Information Law*. Vol. 14. October, 1995. http://www.leepfrog.com/E-Law/Revising.html

Lu, Kathleen. Technological Challenges to Artists' Rights in the Age of Multimedia: The Future Role of Moral Rights. *RSR Reference Services Review*. 22:1 (1994) p9-19.

Lutzker, Arnold. Review and Analysis of the Report of the Working Group on Intellectual Property Rights, Intellectual Property and the National Information Infrastructure (White Paper). Prepared for the Association of Research Libraries, American Library Association, American Association of Law Libraries, Medical Library Association, Special Libraries Association. September 20, 1995. http://www.nlc-bnc.ca/ifla/documents/infopol/copyright/ipwp-rev.txt

Lyman, Peter. "Copyright and Fair Use in the Digital Age: Q and A with Peter Lyman." *Educom Review*. January/February, 1995. http://www.educom.edu/web/ pubs/review/reviewArticles/30132.html

Martin, Peter. Pre-Digital Law: How Prior Information Technologies Have Shaped Access to and the Nature of Law. Montréal: Centre de recherche en droit public (CRDP). Crown copyright in Cyberspace. May 12, 1995. http://www.droit.umontreal. ca/crdp/en/equipes/technologie/conferences/dac/index.html

Massarsky, Barry M. The Operating Dynamics Behind ASCAP, BMI and SESAC, The U.S. Performing Rights Societies. n.d. http://www.nlc-bnc.ca/ifla/documents/ infopol/copyright/massarsk.txt

MIT. "Ethics and Law on the Electronic Frontier." http://www-swiss.ai.mit.edu/6095/ index.html

Moore, June B. Copyrighting Public Domain Programs. http://www.nlc-bnc.ca/ifla/ documents/infopol/copyright/moore.txt

National Writers Union. Statement of Principles on Contracts between Writers and Electronic Book Publishers. April, 1994. http://www.ilt.columbia.edu/projects/ copyright/papers/NWU/NWU1.html

National Writers Union. Recommended Principles for Contracts Covering Online Book Publishing. September, 1994. http://www.nlc-bnc.ca/ifla/documents/info-pol/copyright/nwu2.htm

Negroponte, Nicholas. Bill of Writes. *Wired* Issue 3.05 (May 1995). http://www.hotwired.com/wired/3.05/departments/negroponte.html

Nelson, Theodor Holm. A Publishing and Royalty Model for Networked Documents. n.d. http://www.nlc-bnc.ca/ifla/documents/infopol/copyright/nelson.txt

Norderhaug, Terje and Oberding, Juliet M. "Designing a Web of Intellectual Property." Computer Networks and ISDN Systems, 27:6 (1995). pp. 1037-46. http://www.ifi.uio.no/~terjen/pub/webip/950220.html

Oakley, Robert L. Copyright and Preservation: A Serious Problem in Need of a Thoughtful Solution. The Commission on Preservation and Access. September, 1990. gopher://palimpsest.stanford.edu:70/00/ByOrg/CPA/Reports/oakley.txt

Oakley, Robert L. Statement on Behalf of Several Library and Education Associations. Working Group on Intellectual Property of the Information Policy Committee of the National Information Infrastructure Task Force. November 18, 1993. http://www.nlc-bnc.ca/ifla/documents/infopol/copyright/oakley2.txt

Oakley, Robert L. Statement on Behalf of American Association of Law Libraries and Several Other Library Organizations. Working Group on Intellectual Property of the Information Policy Committee of the National Information Infrastructure Task Force. September 22, 1994. http://www.nlc-bnc.ca/ifla/documents/infopol/copyright/oakley1.txt

Okerson, Ann. Panel Discussion: Intellectual Properties Issues. Association of Research Libraries. http://www.nlc-bnc.ca/ifla/documents/infopol/copyright/okerson.htm

Oppenheim, Charles. LISLEX: Legal Issues of Concern to the Library and Information Sector. *Journal of Information Science.* 21: 4 (1995) p: 300-304.

Perritt, Henry W., Jr. Knowbots, Permissions Headers and Contract Law. April, 1993. http://www.nlc-bnc.ca/ifla/documents/infopol/copyright/perh2.txt

Perrit, Henry, Jr. Protection of Intellectual Property in the National Information Infrastructure. Statement to the Working Group on Intellectual Property of the Information Policy Committee of the National Information Infrastructure (NII) Task Force. c1993. http://www.nlc-bnc.ca/ifla/documents/infopol/copyright/perh1.txt

Phillips, Kenneth L. Meta-Information, The Network of the Future and Intellectual Property Protection. n.d. http://www.nlc-bnc.ca/ifla/documents/infopol/copyright/phillips.txt

Picture Agency Council of America. "The Copyright Commandments from PACA." http://www.indexstock.com/pages/pacacrl.htm

Richards, David. The Copyright Law and the Musician. June, 1990. http://www.nlc-bnc.ca/ifla/documents/infopol/copyright/ricd.txt

Saffo, Paul. It's the Context, Stupid. *Wired* Online Service. 1994. http://www.nlc-bnc.ca/ifla/documents/infopol/copyright/safp1.htm

Samuelson, Pamela. The Copyright Grab. http://www.hotwired.com/wired/whitepaper.html

Samuelson, Pamela. Digital Media and the Law. *Communications of the ACM.* October, 1991. http://www.eff.org/pub/Intellectual_property/digital_media_and_law.paper

Samuelson, Pamela. First Amendment Rights for Information Providers. *Communications of the ACM.* 34:6 (June, 1991) p19ss. http://www.eff.org/pub/Intellectual_property/first_amend_rights_for_info_providers.paper

Samuelson, Pamela. Intellectual Property Rights and the Global Information Economy. *Communications of the ACM.* 39:1 (Jan. 1996) p. 23-28.

Samuelson, Pamela. Is Information Property? *Communications of the ACM.* 34:3 (March 1991). p15ss. http://www.eff.org/pub/Intellectual_property/is_info_property.paper

Samuelson, Pamela. The Never-Ending Struggle for Balance. *Communications of the ACM* 40:5 (May, 1997) p. 17-21.

Samuelson, Paula. "Legally Speaking: The NII Intellectual Property Report." *Communications of the ACM.* (December, 1994). http://www.ilt.columbia.edu/projects/copyright/papers/samuelson2.html

Samuelson, Paula. Copyright, Digital Data, and Fair Use in Digital Networked Environments. Centre de recherche en droit public (CRDP). The Electronic Superhighway. Montreal: May 13th 1994. http://www.droit.umontreal.ca/crdp/en/equipes/technologie/conferences/dac/index.html

Samuelson, Paula. Copyright Law and Electronic Compilations of Data. *Communications of the ACM.* 35:n2 (February, 1992). p27ss. http://www.eff.org/pub/Intellectual_property/ ip_and_electronic_data.paper

Schlacter, Eric. "Intellectual Property Protection Regimes in the Age of the Internet." Palo Alto, CA. http://blake.oit.unc.edu/copyright1.html

Shade, Leslie Regan. Copyright in the Digital Networked Environment. Discussion Paper for Intellectual Property or Public Knowledge: A Roundtable Discussion of Copyright in the Nineties. Concordia University. April 7, 1995. http://www.nlc-bnc.ca/ifla/documents/infopol/copyright/shade01.htm

Shneiderman, Ben. Protecting Rights in User Interface Designs. Prepared for *ACM SIGCHI Bulletin* October, 1990. *http://www.nlc-bnc.ca/ifla/documents/infopol/ copyright/shnb.txt* gopher://wiretap.spies.com:70/00/Library/Article/Rights/userintf.cp

Smallson, Fran. Soliciting from a Spectrum of Sources. *Intellectual Property Magazine* (February, 1995). http://www.nlc-bnc.ca/ifla/documents/infopol/copyright/smaf1.htm

Stallman, Richard M. Copywrong. Gopher://info.asu.edu/00/asu-cwis/pub-progs/com457/Readings/stallman

Stanbury, William T. "Aspects of Public Policy Regarding Crown Copyright in the Digital Age." Centre de recherche en droit public (CRDP). Crown copyright in Cyberspace. Montréal. May 12, 1995. http://www.droit.umontreal.ca/crdp/en/equipes/technologie/conferences/dac/index.html

Sterling, J.A. "Crown Copyright in the United Kingdom and Other Commonwealth Countries." Crown copyright in Cyberspace Conference. CRDP. Crown copyright in Cyberspace. Montréal. May 12, 1995. http://www.droit.umontreal.ca/crdp/en/equipes/technologie/conferences/dac/index.html

Strong, William S. Copyright in the New World of Electronic Publishing. Presented at the workshop Electronic Publishing Issues II at the Association of American University Presses (AAUP) Annual Meeting, June 17, 1994, Washington, D.C. *Journal of Electronic Publishing.* http://www.press.umich.edu/jep/works/strong.copyright.html

Stuart, Linda. Copyright Rules Updated for the 'Net. *Info World Canada.* 22:2 (Feb., 1997) p. 12.

Talab, R. S. An Educational Use Checklist for Copyright and Multimedia. *Tech-Trends*. 42:1 (Jan-Feb 1997) p9-11.

Talab, Rosemary. Copyright and Multimedia, Part Two: Higher Education. *Tech Trends*. 40:1 (Jan-Feb 1995) p8-10.

Templeton, Brad. Copyright Myths FAQ. Accessed 8/7/00. http://www.clari.net/brad/copymyths.html

Upthegrove, Luella and Roberts, Tom. Intellectual Property Header Descriptors: A Dynamic Approach. http://www.nlc-bnc.ca/ifla/documents/infopol/copyright/uptl.txt

USENET. Copyright FAQ. http://www.lib.ox.ac.uk/internet/news/faq/by_category.law.copyright-faq.html

U.S. NTIA. Virtual Conference on Universal Access and Open Service. November 1994.

_____ Bower, James M. Intellectual Property and the Information Infrastructure. http://www.nlc-bnc.ca/ifla/documents/infopol/copyright/jbower.txt

_____ Henderson, Carol C. A Balancing Act: Copyright in the Electronic Age. http://www.nlc- bnc.ca/ifla/documents/infopol/copyright/chender.txt

Van-Bergen, Marilyn A. Copyright Law, Fair Use, and Multimedia. EDUCOM Review. 27:4 (Jul-Aug 1992) p31-34.

Various. Statement on Lawful Uses of Copyrighted Works. http://www.nlc-bnc.ca/ifla/documents/infopol/copyright/uses.htm

Vaver, David. "Copyright and the State in Canada and the United States." Centre de recherche en droit public (CRDP). Crown copyright in Cyberspace. Montréal. May 12, 1995. http://www.droit.umontreal.ca/CRDP/Conferences/DAC/VAVER/VAVER.html

What's Fair? A Report on the Proceedings of the National Conference on Educational Fair Access and the New Media. Washington, DC. June 15-17, 1994. Agency for Instructional Technology, Bloomington, IN. 1994.

DOA at the Online Ramp

Leah Theriault

To say that the fair use doctrine has been gradually narrowed in recent years by the "market-centric"[1] approach to the defense is relatively uncontroversial. What currently remains of the doctrine, and its probable future, are much more open to debate. My contention, perhaps given away by my rather colorful title, is that fair use will have no room to operate on the Internet[2] of the very near future, and little room to operate in more traditional arenas. In support of my rather dire predictions, I will offer answers to two simple but crucial questions: (1) What are the present and future threats to the fair use doctrine; and (2) What are the possible sources of revitalization of the fair use defense? My answers to these questions unfortunately lead me to the conclusion that fair use is a defense with little wind left in its sails, both on and off the Internet. Despite these pessimistic conclusions, however, I will end this short essay with a rather bold assertion of the drastic steps needed to breathe new life into the doctrine.[3] For although I foretell destruction like a prophet wailing at the gates of the city, I am a pragmatist above all things, and cannot bear to bemoan anything without offering a possible solution to the problem.

OF MEANS AND ENDS: COPYRIGHT AND THE CONSTITUTION

Before embarking on my analysis, however, some preliminary explanation of both the fair use defense and the purposes of the Copy-

Leah Theriault is a student-at-law, McMillan Binch, Suite 3800, South Tower Royal Bank Plaza, Tornot, Canada M5J 2J7. She admits sole responsibility for all opinions expressed in this essay. Any errors or omissions are also her own.

[Haworth co-indexing entry note]: "DOA at the Online Ramp." Theriault, Leah. Co-published simultaneously in *The Acquisitions Librarian* (The Haworth Information Press, an imprint of The Haworth Press, Inc.) No. 26, 2001, pp. 61-88; and: *Publishing and the Law: Current Legal Issues* (ed: A. Bruce Strauch) The Haworth Information Press, an imprint of The Haworth Press, Inc., 2001, pp. 61-88. Single or multiple copies of this article are available for a fee from The Haworth Document Delivery Service [1-800-342-9678, 9:00 a.m. - 5:00 p.m. (EST). E-mail address: getinfo@haworthpressinc.com].

right Act is in order. The Patent and Copyright clause of the Constitution enables Congress to enact laws that "Promote the Progress of Science and Useful Arts."[4] The Copyright Act was enacted under this grant of power, and so is ostensibly meant to serve this Constitutional purpose. The Constitution goes further than this, however, and offers some specific guidelines on how this goal is to be achieved: "by securing for limited Times to Authors and Inventors the exclusive Right to their respective Writings and Discoveries."[5] The Constitutional grounding of the Copyright Act is important, for it establishes that a copyright is a functional monopoly, meant to serve the dominant purpose of promoting social progress. The reward to the author is the *method* used to achieve this purpose; it is not itself the *purpose* of the state grant. In addition to the limits imposed by the Constitution, the case of *Wheaton v. Peters*[6] dispelled any lingering doubts about the importance of rewarding authors in American copyright law, deciding that copyright law is exclusively grounded in state grant, and has no independent "natural rights" status. The distinction between the "natural rights" and "state grant" conceptions of copyright law is critical, for it determines the baseline assumptions against which the provisions of the Copyright Act must be measured. In the case of the "natural rights" conception, the starting point is the absolute right of the author to his creation, and to the monetary rewards from the exploitation of that creation.[7] Any derogation from this starting point is correctly seen as a subsidy moving from the creator to the public. In the case of the "state grant" conception of copyright, the starting point is the absolute freedom of ideas and the unrestricted movement and use of physical copies of creative works. The copyright monopoly, which places restrictions on works after they have passed into the hands of the public,[8] must be justified against the backdrop of this state grant. In this second conception, the copyright is a grant rather than a right, and so is really a subsidy granted by the state to the author. To the extent that this state grant falls short of an absolute property right, as when fair use operates, the shortfall cannot be properly referred to as a subsidy moving from authors to the public.

The copyright subsidy is designed to overcome the "public goods" and "non-appropriability" problems associated with creative works: creative works require a large up-front investment cost, but they are easily and cheaply copied by others once they are released for public consumption. This makes it difficult for an author to recoup his investment costs, and so makes the initial investment more risky, and less attractive, from the author's point of view. The law makes the initial creative investment less risky–and thus more likely to occur–by prohibiting others from reaping the monetary rewards from the creative work for a specified length of time. This incentive story lies at the heart of American copyright law, but it is fundamentally deficient in several respects. Its prime shortcoming is that it does not tell us "how much" guaranteed monetary reward is required to convince the author to create.[9] In addition, the insulating circularity of the rationale makes it easy to lose sight of both the ultimate goal of the copyright grant, and of the situations in which the incentive story begins to disserve that ultimate goal. Giving the creator too much control over his work after it has passed into the hands of the public can threaten freedom of speech, hamper scholarship and learning, and adversely affect the ability of other artists and authors to create new works. These results disserve the Constitutional goal of promoting social progress just as much as incentive-destroying free-riding does.

The status of a copyright as (1) a state grant (2) meant to serve a specific Constitutional purpose, is essential to a proper understanding of American copyright law, for these factors shape both the means and the ends of the Copyright Act. These defining characteristics demand that the provisions of the Copyright Act achieve the specific result of promoting progress in science and the arts. Thus, the grant of exclusive rights to the copyright owner in § 106, and the fair use defense in § 107, must both serve this purpose. There should be no doubt that this is so after the Supreme Court's unequivocal statement in *Sony*: "The monopoly privileges that Congress may authorize are neither unlimited nor primarily designed to provide a special private benefit. Rather, the limited grant is a means by which an important public purpose may be achieved."[10] What this means at a practical level is that the provisions of the Copyright Act are not carved in stone: they are at all times subject to the scrutiny of the Constitutional purpose, and should be applied in a manner consistent with that purpose. They should also be altered if they stop serving this Constitutional purpose. Judges have long given implicit recognition to this fact, for the fair use defense itself arose out of a judicial recognition that the copyright monopoly was impeding, rather than promoting, the creative endeavor. Applied strictly, the exclusive rights posed the danger of stifling learning and authorship, both of which require users to draw on the work of their predecessors. This judge-made doctrine operated as a defense in those cases in which the courts thought that the public benefit of the infringement outweighed the private cost of refusing to grant relief to the copyright owner, and was not codified until the passage of the 1976 Act. Ironically, the judiciary that created the fair use defense has also narrowed its application in recent years, mainly via an overzealous embracing of the market harm/market failure rationale of fair use. However, this is not the only threat to the fair use doctrine, as we shall soon see.

THE DECLINE AND FALL OF FAIR USE

Three main developments threaten the existence of a robust fair use defense: (1) the "market-centric" interpretation of fair use; (2) contractual override of fair use; and (3) legislation designed to make mass market licenses of copyrighted works legally enforceable and to make circumvention of technological protection systems illegal. The first of these factors is largely responsible for the present anemic state of the fair use defense, while the last two have the potential to destroy the defense completely. I have not included "technological developments" as a separate category of threat because this factor is so intimately intertwined with the others. Although I will consider each of these developments, I will spend most of my time discussing the first because it arises from within the Act itself, and thus weakens the fair use defense at its roots.

Strike I: The Market-Centric Approach to Copyright

In copyright as in all areas of law, the statute is just the tip of the iceberg: it is judicial interpretation that most often sinks the ship. In order to understand the present state of the fair use defense, then, it is necessary to trace its treatment in the courts. Although this sampling of the cases does not purport to be exhaustive in either breadth or depth, I will canvass those decisions that have had the greatest impact on the doctrine to date. In this section, we'll spend most of our time in the Supreme Court, but make some undoubtedly familiar detours to the ninth and sixth circuits.

The fair use analysis is in all cases fact intensive, and involves consideration of the four statutory factors listed in § 107.[11] These factors are: "(1) the purpose and character of the use . . . ; (2) the nature of the copyrighted work; (3) the amount and substantiality of the portion used in relation to the copyrighted work as a whole; and (4) the effect of the use upon the potential market for or value of the copyrighted work."[12] Although several Supreme Court decisions have stressed the importance of considering all four factors, the ability of these factors to account for the public purpose goals of the Act has been seriously eroded via judicial interpretation and application of the "four-part" test. This erosion has occurred in three ways: first, the fourth factor has assumed paramount importance in several of this country's courts; second, two out of the remaining three factors have been functionally transformed into market harm tests by the judiciary; and third, several courts have adopted a "market failure" rationale of fair use. These three developments have combined to seriously narrow the scope of the doctrine.

The Beginning of the End:
Harper *and the Supremacy of the Market Harm Factor*

Harper & Row Publishers, Inc. v. Nation Enterprises[13] is one of those cases in which you know the court reached the right result for the wrong reasons.[14] The case involved the publication of President Ford's memoirs, which included a much awaited account of his pardon of President Nixon. Harper & Row had signed a prepublication agreement with *Time Magazine*, in which Harper licensed the right to quote from the book's account of the pardon. The value of this prepublication agreement was severely diminished when *The Nation* newspaper preempted *Time* and published its own quotes from the forthcoming novel. *Time* subsequently refused to pay the outstanding balance on its prepublication agreement with Harper. Although there is much discussion in the case of "illegal sources" and "purloined manuscripts," *Nation* was never found to have stolen the manuscript, and most likely possessed it for purposes of publishing a review in its newspaper, or supplying a promotional quote for the cover of the book. The practice of supplying commentators with prepublication copies of book manuscripts in the hope of obtaining some favorable promotional quotes is standard industry practice. It is unfortunate that the Court did not try to more explicitly factor the maintenance of industry practice into the fair use analysis; instead, the Court chose to make a blanket statement that the market harm to the original work was the single most important factor in the fair use analysis. It is easy to see why the Court placed so much emphasis on the market harm factor in this case: it was virtually the only factor on which they could base a finding of liability. Although *Nation*'s use of the material was commercial, it was also for news reporting, a use traditionally considered to be at the core of both fair use and free speech. The work was also factual in nature, and dealt with matters of national importance, so the "nature of the copyrighted work" also cut against Harper. Finally, *Nation*'s quotations were quantitatively insubstantial in relation to the length of the book. Under these circumstances, the Court did what it could to maintain a finding of liability: it stressed the commercial rather than the news reporting aspect of the use; it highlighted the qualitative importance of the excerpts which *Nation* had published (the pardon was the most, if not the only, sensational portion of the book); and it stated that: "[the fourth] factor is undoubtedly the single most important element of fair use."[15]

Harper left us with three damaging legacies. The first is its statement that the market harm factor is the most important in the fair use analysis. Although the Court retreated from this strong statement in a subsequent case,[16] we shall see below that its legacy lives on in the circuit courts. The second is its reference to, and apparent approval of, the market failure rationale of fair use.[17] This rationale also lives on in the circuit courts, and the Supreme Court has not yet specifically disclaimed it. The third is its determination that: "the fair use doctrine was predicated on the author's implied consent to 'reasonable and customary' use when he released his work for public consumption."[18] Although this formulation has not had a major impact in the courts to date, and has even been used by one circuit court judge in an admirable effort to support a finding of fair use,[19] it could destroy fair use completely if we were to take it seriously. It is already difficult to entertain the fiction that publishers consent to any unpaid, unauthorized use of their works, even if those uses are considered by onlookers to be "reasonable and customary." This fiction would be even more difficult to maintain in a world of click-through contracts and micro-payments, in which there is the possibility of compensation for, and contractual definition of, virtually every use. We can admire the Court's attempt in *Harper* to recognize the greater unfairness that arises when a second author uses material from the first author's unpublished work, but the Court did not need to take the extra step of accepting the "implied consent" formulation of fair use. Although there was support in the literature for such a formulation,[20] it quite literally does not make sense. If the fair use defense had anything to do with the implied consent of publishers or copyright owners, it would not have been created by the judiciary to deny relief to copyright owners during infringement proceedings. What fair use is designed to do, of course, is determine when an unpaid use is reasonable despite a painfully obvious lack of consent.

No Fair: Campbell v. Acuff-Rose and the 75% Market Harm Test

Acuff-Rose sued 2 Live Crew for producing a rather bawdy rap take-off of Roy Orbison's famous song, Pretty Woman. 2 Live Crew defended on the basis that its version of Pretty Woman was a parody of the original, and thus fell under the umbrella of criticism, which is specifically listed as a protected use in § 107. The Supreme Court decided that, as a general matter, parody was indeed entitled to the protection of the fair use defense, stating that there is no "protecible derivative market for criticism."[21] However, the Court also stated that a parody was subject to the rigors of the four-factor test. Like any other work, a parody must be dissected to make sure that the parodist did not take "too much" of the original. At first glance, this makes sense: infringers should not be able to copy works virtually wholesale and forgo the need to pay a licensing fee, simply by throwing in a jab or two to make it look like they are making fun of the original. However, at a practical level, this test runs the danger of forcing courts to engage in the type of aesthetic discrimination long eschewed by the courts.[22] A parody is meant to make fun of another work, so it must copy enough of that original work to identify it as the parodic target, a fact which the Court was careful to acknowledge. At the same time, the parody must not take so much from the original that it constitutes a disguised act of copying. This requires that the "purely copied" elements be separated from the "copied for parody" elements. The identification of an element as "parodic" requires a judgement of its critical content, and this judgement may depend to a large extent on the analyst's reaction to the work. It may therefore be that the line between "parodies" and "copies" is coincident with the line between "good" and "bad" parodies, regardless of efforts to the contrary.

Despite the difficulties inherent in sifting the parodists from the copiers, *Campbell* did contain several elements favorable to the fair use defense. It recognized the social value of criticism and the role of fair use in promoting such commentary, and refused to entertain a market failure vision of criticism, stating that an unauthorized parody was fair use even when the copyright owner would have agreed to license. Furthermore, it removed most of the presumption of unfairness for commercial uses that was set up in *Sony*.[23] I say that "most" of the presumption was removed, because the presumption that "mere duplication for commercial purposes" is unfair appears to remain. The Supreme Court's refusal to adopt a blanket presumption against fair use for commercial works was based upon both the text of the Act itself, and commercial reality. As regards the latter factor, the court was exactly on target when it quoted Samuel Johnson: "[n]o man but a blockhead ever wrote except for money."[24] Critics need to eat just as much as authors do, and criticism of creative works would be infrequent if the critics, parodists, and commentators of the world could not get paid for their efforts. As regards the Supreme Court's textual argument against presumptions, it is quite correct that there is no basis in the statute for treating any one of the four factors listed in §§ 107 (1)-(4) as more important–and hence deserving of a presumption for or against fair use–than the others. However, this textual argument against presumptions for the "four factors" does not necessarily extend to the specific examples listed in the main body of § 107, a point to which I will return later. It is therefore unfortunate that, in its haste to dismantle the commercial/non-commercial presumptions set out in *Sony*, the Supreme Court found it necessary to conclude that no presumption of fairness was warranted for the factors enumerated in the main body of § 107.

Campbell was in many ways the courts "housekeeping" case, because it gave the Court the chance to repudiate both its presumptions in *Sony* and its statement in *Harper* that the market harm factor was the most important in the fair use analysis. In addition, its statement that there is no protectible derivative market for criticism, although it was quite a limited statement of principle, could possibly be used to support a more general rejection of the market failure rationale in future cases. All of these developments were certainly positive from the point of view of fair use advocates. Unfortunately, however, *Campbell* may have actually done more harm than good to § 107, via its interpretation of the "purpose and character" arm of the fair use analysis, and its insistence that parodies be subjected to a modified market harm test. It is to these issues which I now turn.

The Purpose of the Purpose Test

In speaking of the first factor of the fair use analysis, the Court in *Campbell* said the following: "The central purpose of this investigation is to see, in Justice Story's words, whether the new work merely 'supercede[s] the objects' of the original creation . . . or instead adds something new, with a further purpose or different character . . . whether and to what extent the new work is transformative."[25] Although the Court was careful to point out that transformation is not absolutely necessary for a finding of fair use, it did state that a non-transformative work will have more difficulty in qualifying for the fair use exemption: "the more transformative the new work, the less will be the significance of other factors, like commercialism, that may weigh against a finding of fair use."[26] Unfortunately, parsing the first factor as a "superceding the objects of the original" test transforms the first factor into a market substitution test. There is a double harm inflicted here: the practical weight of the market harm factor is increased, and the ability of the first factor to effectively account for the public purposes of the use is virtually destroyed. In fact, this reinterpretation of the first prong is the most damaging to fair use, for the purpose and character test is the only factor that allows consideration of the public benefits of various uses to enter into the fair use analysis. When this interpretation of the first arm is combined with the Court's use of the "amount" factor in § 107(3) to assess both the first and the fourth prongs, the Act's "four factor" test is functionally transformed into a 75% market harm test.

The Court's use of Justice Story's discussion of the infringement factors in the *Folsom v. Marsh*[27] case is unfortunate, for that case involved a commercial work which used substantial excerpts from another copyrighted work. The court was therefore exclusively concerned with the market effect of the second publication on the original, and it did not contemplate the notion of the other public purposes fulfilled by the fair use defense. In addition, with respect to opinions to the contrary, I think that Justice Story's words indicate that the "supercede the objects of the original" language was clearly a market harm, and not a purpose, test: "[W]e must . . . look to the nature and objects of the selections made, the quantity and value of the materials used, *and* the degree in which the use may prejudice the sale, *or* diminish the profits, *or* supercede the objects, of the original work."[28] (Emphasis added.)

That's Not Funny: The Modified Market Harm Test

The purpose of a parody is ridicule, and effective ridicule may completely destroy the market for the parodied work. For this reason, the Court stated that market harm to the original work is not remediable; however, the Court did determine that the market harm inflicted by the parody on the market for rap derivatives was potentially remediable. The Court was careful to point out that harm to the market for rap derivatives that arises from the effectiveness of the song's "parodic element" will not be remediable under the Act. However, how is a parodist supposed to prove that harm occurs from the effectiveness of the parody rather than from the status of a parody as a substitute for rap derivatives? Recall that fair use is an affirmative defense, so the infringer will carry the burden of showing that there is no remediable market harm. In most cases, it will be impossible for such fine distinctions to be proven by even the most meticulously gathered evidence. It may be that the Supreme Court has unintentionally erected a hurdle which no parodist can clear.[29] In addition to the difficulty of bearing the evidentiary burden, it is not at all clear why it should matter that a parody damages potential revenues from potential derivative works. If the court felt that derivative works were sufficiently distinct from the original work that their harm would occur independently of the harm to the original, then harm to the derivative work will always be compensable. A parody takes aim at the original work, so independent derivative works could, by definition, not be harmed by "the parodic element" of that parody. If, on the other hand, the Court felt that derivative works were sufficiently connected to the original work that they, too, could be harmed by a parody taking aim at the original, then harm to derivative works will never be compensable. Quite clearly, then, subjecting a parody to any form of market harm test does not make sense.

The Market Failure Rationale: PUP v. MDS and Texaco v. AGU

The market failure rationale of fair use may have had its first bit-part in *Harper*, but it had the starring role in two recent Appeal Court cases. The first of these was *American Geophysical Union v. Texaco, Inc.*,[30] in which the Court decided that a corporate scientist could not make fair use archival copies of his company's scientific journal subscription, despite the fact that he only copied one or two articles from each journal, and the fact that his employer paid the corporate rate for each individual copy of the journal.[31] This case was unequivocal in its adoption of the market failure rationale: "[I]t is not unsound to conclude that the right to seek payment for a particular use tends to become legally cognizable under the fourth fair use factor when the means for paying for such a use is made easier. This notion is not inherently troubling: it is sensible that a particular unauthorized use should be considered 'more fair' when there is no ready market or means to pay for the use, while such an unauthorized use should be considered 'less fair' when there is a ready market or means to pay for the use."[32] The Court went even further than this, however, stating that "only traditional, reasonable *or likely to be developed* markets"[33] would be considered in the market harm analysis under the fourth factor. Although the Court was careful to point out that its refusal to find fair use was based upon the specific facts of the case, and that there was a reasonably functioning market for the collection of photocopying license fees in this case, it is difficult to know how seriously to take the Court's comment about markets that are *likely* to be developed.[34] If the market failure rationale extends, not only to existing markets, but also to markets that are likely to be developed, then the scope of fair use is diminished to the vanishing point. The Court did not explain what its conception of "likely to be developed" was, but it may very well be that the monitoring and incremental payment systems envisioned by copyright owners and digital publishers are sufficiently "likely" to be developed that there is legally no room for fair use of digital works.[35]

The second case which explicitly espoused the market failure rationale was *Princeton University Press v. Michigan Document Services*: "Where, on the other hand, the copyright owner clearly does have an interest in exploiting a licensing market–and especially where the copyright owner has actually succeeded in doing so–it is appropriate that potential revenues for photocopying be considered in a fair use analysis."[36] *MDS* is especially troubling for the educational arm of fair use because it involved the preparation of course packs for students. In addition, the actual market harm suffered by the copyright owners was not as clear as the Court's focus on the Copyright Clearance Center made it seem. Often if an excerpt is not photocopied for students, it will be put on reserve so that the students can photocopy it themselves. Does the result in *MDS* imply that this practice, when done by the students individually, is also not fair use? Certainly, the market effect when students copy the material for themselves is the same as when the copy shop does the copying for them. In fact, if a professor has a choice between: (1) putting a book on reserve so that students can photocopy parts of it; (2) sending the excerpt to a copy shop so that copies can be made for all of the students at once; and (3) omitting the material from the syllabus because students cannot afford to buy all of the books or articles that would be useful for them to read; then there is no market harm to the copyright owner because there is no lost sale. The irony of the market harm analysis is, that once we consider potential harm to potential markets, there is no such thing as a use that has a "noncommercial" *effect*. The use itself creates a market that the copyright owner could potentially exploit. There are, however, noncommercial end *uses*, and this should be the focus of the analysis.

MDS is also troubling for what did not happen in the case. Specifically, the case did not go on to the Supreme Court, but was denied certiorari in 1997. There were two issues which the Supreme Court might have thought important enough to settle despite the lack of a Circuit split on the issue of photocopying fair use: (1) the meaning of "multiple copies for classroom use" in § 107; and (2) the *MDS* majority's apparent disbelief that *Campbell* had reversed *Harper's* statement that the fourth factor deserved the most weight in the fair use analysis. In discussing the fourth factor, the majority made the following comments: "The four statutory factors may not have been created equal. In determining whether a use is 'fair,' the Supreme Court has said that the most important factor is the fourth . . ." (but see *American Geophysical Union v. Texaco Inc.*, suggesting that the Supreme Court may now have abandoned the idea that the fourth factor is of paramount importance).[37] The odd result of the Supreme Court's decision in *Sony Corp. v. Universal City Studios, Inc.*,[38] and its denial of certiorari in the *MDS* case, is that a VCR manufacturer can assist a television viewer to record copyrighted audiovisual works, but a copy service cannot assist students and scholars to obtain photocopies of research and educational material without incurring copyright liability. To the extent that one thinks that the latter uses are more closely aligned with the progress of science and the arts, this result appears to turn the Constitutional purpose of the Copyright Act on its head. This result is also unfortunate because there is no principled reason to differentiate between a company that aids infringement by selling a product, and a company that aids infringement by directly providing a service. The fact that fair use would stand or fall on such a distinction rather misses the point of the defense: the important question should be the end use of the infringing copies, not the form in which the intermediary offers its services to the user. Surely the Constitutional purposes of the Copyright Act demand, at the very least, that the fair use determination should not be a game of "pin the tail on the infringer."

Strike II: Fair Use and Contractual Override

The market failure rationale erodes the fair use defense from within the Copyright Act itself; not surprisingly, however, there are also threats outside of the Act. Contract law is a formidable adversary for even a Constitutionally-based law like copyright, for contract law is premised on individual freedom and the free market system. The legal system is loathe to interfere with private agreements, because these agreements express the free will of the parties. Private agreements also express the will of the market, and the market allocates resources more efficiently than state mandate. The revered status of the contractual agreement leads to an obvious question: If a copyright owner does not want her works to be subject to the "free use" result that accompanies a successful fair use defense, then why doesn't she simply get the user to agree to pay for all uses? There are two answers to this question. First, of course, copyright owners have done this before–they have probably even done it to you. Second, the bargain theory of contract law places internal limits on the enforceability of contracts.[39] If a contract does not express the will of the parties, then the reasons for enforcing it do not exist. It is important to note that the "will of the parties" refers to the "will of the parties when the bargain was struck": if you change your mind later, for example, your fickleness will not let you renege on your contractual promise.

Contract formation is a problem for copyright owners because most of their products are sold for mass consumption, and so the would-be contracting parties never even get a chance to meet, let alone form a nuanced bargain which disclaims fair use rights. Copyright owners have sought to remedy this problem by using "shrink-wrap" or "click-through" contracts. These contracts are typed in micro-pitch on the outside of a box of software, or are largely hidden in a pop-up window which appears when you load software into your machine for the first time. These "agreements" usually tell you that you agree to a great number of restrictions on the use of the product which you just bought, and they might tell you that you should return the product to get your money back if you don't agree to these restrictions. This method of contract formation is somewhat troublesome for contract law, because the terms of the contract were not known to you at the time of purchase. It is therefore difficult to speak of your "agreement" to them. The unilateral imposition of complex terms after the "bargain" is struck is normally not allowed in contract law, and the "bargain" that we call a "sale" is normally concluded at the time of purchase.[40] The legal enforceability of such contracts has thus always been subject to some doubt. However, "standard form" contracts–contracts which accompany mass market goods, and which contain provisions which are rarely read by the purchaser–are commonly enforced by the courts for many types of goods. Essentially, the courts strain the concept of a contract and enforce these "add-on" and "hidden" agreements because mass marketing and distribution make it impossible for contracts to be formed in the "simultaneously bilateral" manner contemplated by traditional contract law. In the case of software, however, most courts have historically declined to enforce these "after-the-fact" agreements.[41] This trend may be changing, however, as a more recent Seventh Circuit decision found, not only that these contracts were enforceable, but that they were enforceable even when they conflicted with the terms of the Copyright Act.[42] Although courts have not yet ruled on the enforceability of a click-through contract, it may be that these agreements are more likely to be enforced than their shrink-wrap counterparts, since the user must undertake what appears to be a positive act of assent, by clicking the "Yes" or "I Agree" box on the screen. And although most of these contracts have been applied to software up to the present time, they can be encoded into any digital "good," whether it be a CD to be downloaded, or a web site to be visited.

A Note on Technological Protection Systems

There are essentially two ways for a copyright owner to remedy the uncertainties inherent in the contractual protection of digitally-rendered works. The vagaries of judicial interpretation can be circumvented by legislative fiat, or the contractual mechanism of protection can be abandoned in favor of a more high-tech solution. Of course, these two methods are not mutually exclusive, as the example of the click-through contract clearly shows. Computer code is truly the multi-purpose gadget of the future: it can be used to render the copyrighted work, to place contractual terms on the work where they must be assented to in order to gain access to the work, and, for those users who insist on denying their previous evidence of contractual intent, prevent unauthorized copying of the work. There are various ways that this can be accomplished, but the technological specifics are not relevant to this discussion. The important thing here is the fact that technology can be used both to enhance (in the case photocopiers and computers) and hamper (in the case of embedded code) the unauthorized copying of works. Technological protection systems can operate in isolation of traditional methods of enforcing the will of the copyright owner, or they can assist the contractual protection of copyrighted works by overcoming the privity problem. If the contract appears each time a work is accessed, each user can be bound to its terms. Of course, the validity of the contract is still dependent upon judicial enforcement, unless the law or the technology steps in and usurps the judicial function. The law, of course, operates by making certain contracts legally enforceable, technology operates by making the law obsolete. It is not improbable that the bulk of future copyright disputes will be decided in the homes of infringers rather than in the court of law, as digital meltdowns occur in response to attempts to copy the work or tamper with the protection system itself–or even after each viewing or use of the work. You might call this the "Maxwell Smart" version of copyright enforcement.

Of course, enforcement of a copyright does not equal enforcement of the Copyright Act, for the Copyright Act places limits on the copyright monopoly, limits which are likely to be ignored by copyright owners interested in extracting the full value of their "copyrights." I use quotations here because the privately enforced version of "copyright" may go so far beyond the statutory grant provided by the Copyright Act, that it should not be referred to as a copyright at all. The limits mandated by the Act include the fair use right, but also encompass scope issues, such as the long-standing principle that facts are not eligible for copyright protection.[43] The real power of the "technological solution" is that it can use the guise of the Copyright Act to leverage a private expansion of the traditional copyright monopoly.[44] It can also be used in concert with more traditional enforcement mechanisms, such as contract and legislation, such that each method provides a "fail-safe" for the others. Thus, for example, if a technological protection system fails to prevent copying, the digitally rendered click-through contract that accompanied the work may be enforced by the courts. Legislation can waterproof this strategy in two ways: it can mandate the enforcement of click-through contracts, and it can prohibit the circumvention of the technological protection mechanisms. This interaction of copyright, contract, technology and law threatens to fundamentally change the way users interact with copyrighted works.

Strike III: "Suppose You Were a Member of Congress . . . ." –Mark Twain

There are three current law-making initiatives particularly relevant to the continued viability of the fair use defense: S. 2037, H.R. 2281 and UCC2B.[45] S. 2037 passed the Senate in May of 1998, while H.R. 2281 passed the House by voice vote on August 4, 1998. The two resulting acts were expected to be reconciled after the House resumes on September 9. The two acts contain various provisions designed to implement the WIPO treaties signed by the Clinton administration in 1996.[46] These acts seek to bolster the protection of copyrights in digital media in the following ways: by prohibiting the manufacture, sale and distribution of devices meant to facilitate the circumvention of technological protection systems; and by making the act of circumvention of technological protection systems illegal. The House act is somewhat more favorable to the fair use defense than its Senate counterpart, in that it includes a review mechanism which would allow the Under Secretary of Commerce for Intellectual Property Policy to waive the prohibition against circumventing a technological protection measure when the otherwise lawful use of "a particular class of copyrighted works" is threatened, particularly when nonprofit libraries, educational institutions or archives are affected. H.R. 2281 also includes a statement that section 1201 does not affect defenses to copyright infringement, including fair use.[47] However, the exceptions and review mechanisms in H.R. 2281 are grossly inadequate, for several reasons. The exemptions depend on periodic review by the

Under Secretary of Commerce for Intellectual Property Policy, the Assistant Secretary of Commerce for Communications and Information and the Registrar of Copyrights, and are thus uncertain of application. More importantly, the exemptions do not extend to the manufacturers, distributors and vendors of circumvention devices, so there may not be easily available methods to circumvent technological protection systems, even to exercise fair use rights. It remains to be seen whether the qualification in 1201 that the circumvention device or service must be "primarily designed or produced for the purposes of circumventing" technological protection measures will be sufficient to provide users with ways to exercise their fair use rights. After all, a device that circumvents a protection system cannot be designed to differentiate between fair and unfair uses, so manufacturers may be dissuaded from developing devices even though they could be used for lawful purposes. Even when a protection system is circumvented, however, the technological protection measure may still fulfill its intended purpose. This is because the very act of circumventing a technological protection system may weigh against a finding of fair use, especially in a court that takes *Harper's* "implied consent" notion of fair use seriously.[48] It is difficult to maintain the fiction of implied consent when the user has taken definite steps to overcome the manifest lack of consent of the copyright owner.

If these were the only sources of inadequacy in H.R. 2281's protection of fair use rights, then fair use might survive on the good graces of the Under Secretary and the technological savvy of librarians, scholars and students. However, there is yet another section of the House and Senate acts which promises an uncertain future for fair use: section 1202, which protects the integrity of copyright management information. Copyright management information is defined in both acts to include things like the name of the author, the title and copyright notice of the work, and the "terms and conditions for use of the work." The acts proscribed by 1202 include the intentional removal of copyright management information, and the distribution of works which you know have had the copyright management information removed. There is a knowledge standard required for criminal penalties under section 1202, and an implied knowledge standard for civil liability, but most people who remove copyright management information, or who know it has been removed by someone else, will at the very least know that the removal of such information will "enable" or "facilitate" infringement. The fact that this is done to exercise fair use rights is no defense here, for there are no explicit exemptions or review mechanisms in the act applicable to section 1202. Recall also that fair use is a defense to activity that would otherwise be an infringement, so removal of copyright management information, even to exercise fair use rights, would violate section 1202. The lack of exemptions for removal of copyright management information is especially troubling when we consider that it maintains the chain of contractual privity by legislative fiat. Copyright management information includes "the terms and conditions for the use of the work": making its removal illegal therefore means that each user will be subject to the will of the copyright owner, *unless courts refuse to enforce a particular contract.* Of course, if the likelihood of judicial non-enforcement is itself decreased significantly by legislative action, then section 1202 will operate to displace the provisions of the very act which it is meant to *protect.* This will occur unless copyright owners voluntarily put "fair use" and "facts aren't covered" clauses in their contracts, or unless the content of the "terms and conditions" of copyright management information is legislatively controlled. At this point in time, both of these possibilities appear to be equally remote. Of course, there is still the problem of judidicial non-enforcement of contractual terms. And this is where UCC2B is designed to come to the aide of the copyright owner.

UCC2B

The technological trick of making the contract stick to the product will not do copyright owners much good if the terms will not stick to the contract. UCC2B seeks to circumvent the bane of judicial interference by giving legislative blessing to the click-through and shrink-wrap methods of contract formation. Not surprisingly, UCC2B is more concerned with ensuring that various methods of "assent by negative implication" will be "judge-proof," than with regulating the content of the contracts themselves. This is not to say that these contracts will never be subject to judicial intervention, for Section 2B-110, as it is now drafted, specifically contemplates the non-enforcement of "unconscionable" terms. A proposed amendment[49] to this section would allow for judicial non-enforcement of terms that are "impermissible" because they are "contrary to public polices relating to innovation, competition, and free expression." Although this is certainly a step forward for consumer protection, the drafters have declined to include an explicit exemption for "fair use" within the text of 2B. Such an amendment was suggested at the May 1997 meeting of the ALI, and is known as the McManis motion. The drafters are adamant, however, that such issues should be dealt with at the federal level. In the end, they may be right that this should be dealt with by Congress. However, one cannot help but wonder when this game of "pass the buck" becomes one of "drop the ball": UCC2B passes it on to Congress, the courts pass it on to Congress, and Congress fumbles the ball. In fact, the drafters of UCC2B seem painfully intent on ignoring the potential for contract law to completely displace Copyright law in its traditional form. Although the drafters briefly discuss the problem of preemption by federal intellectual property law in the most recent draft of the Article, the reporter's statement that "Article 2B deals solely with contract law, not intellectual property, competition, or trade regulation law"[50] is disingenuous, to say the least. If strictly enforced, contract law holds the promise of overwhelming intellectual property law, circumventing competition law and frustrating the purposes of trade agreements. Of course, UCC2B is very much a work in progress, and it is not expected to be ready for adoption by the state legislatures until 2000. Adoption of a clause protective of fair use appears unlikely, however. There is the time, but not the will.

OH WHERE, OH WHERE, HAS THE CONSTITUTION GONE?

The fair use cases speak of balancing interests, but at a practical level, they provide little counterweight to the beguiling circularity of the market failure argument or the overwhelming prominence of the market harm determination. Every policy choice has a cost; the question is who will pay the price. Horse and buggies notwithstanding,[51] there doesn't seem to be any convincing reason to use either the Copyright Act or contract law to ensure that copyright owners maximize their profits, especially when the burden placed on researchers and students is greater, in relative terms, than the burden suffered by the copyright owner from losing some portion of potential profits. Yes, copyright owners need to be rewarded for their investment of time, money and talent. And yes, it is not in society's interest to allow market destructive free-riding by users or competitors. However, loss of potential revenue is not equivalent to destruction of the incentive to create. After all, if the licensing markets that were spawned by the *Kinko's* decision[52] had been crucial to the ability of the copyright grant to operate as an incentive to creation, then the works being copied would not have been published until *after* the photocopying technology had developed. When it can be shown that the copyright owner would be significantly harmed by the infringing activity, such that his incentive to create the work would be destroyed or seriously impaired, then fair use should step aside so that the Copyright Act can perform its incentive function. Otherwise, the fair use defense should operate to balance the public values of education, free speech, research and scholarship with the interest of the copyright owner in compensation. However, the problem with this determination is that copyright owners and judges alike display a distinct lack of prescience in this area. Very few people, for example, could have foreseen the extra profits that would flow to the movie giants from the introduction of the VCR–profits that might have been stifled if the cost of VCRs had been increased by payment of mandatory royalties too soon in the life of this developing market. These difficulties, while palpable, are no excuse for the default answer of "all profits to the copyright owner unless there is some narrow, exceptional public purpose, such as freedom of speech." Ironically, the incentive rationale has reached a natural rights result: all benefits to the creator unless there is some extraordinary reason that they should not flow in this direction.

Looking at the effects on education and research of the extra cost of paying for every copy of a work, even if that copy is only of a portion of the work, is certainly consistent with *Sony's* willingness to look beyond the infringement activity to its effect on the public. There is certainly nothing wrong with balancing the harm to the student and research communities against the incentives to the copyright owner: in fact, the Constitution demands it. Either the Copyright Act is still based on a public purpose rationale, or it has been somehow transformed via judicial interpretation into a modified "natural rights" regime. In order for fair use to survive, we have to separate the issue of commercial use from the issue of the basic right of reproduction. This is complex because the issue of market harm is intertwined with both reproductions per se, and with commercial re-uses. However, if we are going to recognize that the process of learning and education is so intimately tied with both individual thought and social progress, that research and scholarship should not be burdened with the full cost of copyrighted works, then we have to separate commercial reproductions from educational, non-profit reproductions. This would result in a fair use doctrine that protects both "transformative" uses, like news reporting and criticism, and "non-transformative" uses, such as reproductions for classroom use, scholarly analysis and individual study.

GAME OVER? POSSIBLE SOURCES OF REVITALIZATION OF THE FAIR USE DEFENSE

Commentators have both rejoiced at the diminishing role for fair use and called for a rediscovery of its public purpose roots. I, of course, am one of the latter commentators. However, I am more pessimistic than most that this rediscovery can in fact occur. If there is to be a fair use renaissance, the impetus for this renewal must come from either the courts, the law, or "economic default." By "economic default," I refer to the factual, rather than the legal, existence of fair use: it may simply prove too costly or too difficult for copyright owners to enforce their copyrights in the on-line environment. However, the combined effect of new protection technologies and the legal threat of anti-circumvention laws will likely make copyrights easier and cheaper to enforce in the future.[53] In addition, if fair use serves a worthy public purpose, then it should exist *despite* the ability of copyright owners to enforce their copyrights. The law does not appear to be a likely champion of fair use either: the protection for fair use in both H.R. 2281 and S. 2037 is inadequate; while UCC2B seems determined to duck the question. An alternative to the House and Senate acts, H.R. 3048–the proposed Digital Era Copyright Enhancement Act–was introduced in the House on November 13, 1997, but has been languishing in the Subcommittee on Courts and Intellectual Property since the 24th day of that same month. This proposal would have altered the text of both §§ 107 and 301, making it clear that fair use cannot be abrogated by either non-negotiated contracts, or technological protection systems. The House's dismissive treatment of the bill is evidence of the likelihood of legislative revival of the fair use defense.

As the original source of the fair use defense, the courts would seem to be the most likely source of its resurgence. There are three ways in which the courts can bolster the fair use defense: they can discard the market failure vision of fair use in favor of a public purpose conception; they can refuse to enforce non-negotiated contract terms by appealing to contract law principles; or they can declare that certain contract terms are preempted by the Copyright Act. To date, the notion that contract terms can be preempted by the Copyright Act has received short shrift in the courts. The preemption section of the Copyright Act, § 301, only preempts rights that are "equivalent" to the rights set out in § 106. Courts generally use an "extra element" test to determine equivalency, and the prevailing view in the courts appears to be that a contract will generally be sufficiently different from the § 106 rights to pass this extra element test.[54] Another case has gone even further, opining that contracts will *never* be preempted by the Copyright Act.[55] The possibility of setting aside contracts based on contract formation principles may provide no greater respite for the fair use defense. Although the courts have not yet ruled on the enforceability of click-through contracts,[56] shrink-wrap licenses have been held enforceable by at least one court.[57] Furthermore, standard form contracts are routinely held to be valid for many of the products that we purchase everyday, so courts may follow the lead of *ProCD* and uphold contracts for goods in digital form.

Of course, even if courts do decline to enforce non-negotiated contract terms for digital goods, the fair use defense will not be benefited unless courts make a separate determination that the infringing use is fair. Unfortunately, however, this is where we see how the progenitor of the fair use defense has become its greatest threat. Created by the judiciary, the doctrine has been transformed via judicial interpretation into a shadow of its former self. Quite simply, the supremacy of the market harm/market failure rationale of fair use means that there is no longer a convincing argument from within the Copyright Act to defend a broad conception of fair use.

A PRESCRIPTION FOR REVIVAL

Now that I have filled in the death certificate for fair use, I will now have the cheek to write a prescription for its resuscitation. In order for fair use to survive in any recognizable form, some stiff medicine is required. At a bare minimum, the courts must radically alter the way they apply the "four-factor" test of § 107. The courts say that they recognize that fair use has social goals, and that the primary purpose of the copyright act is to serve the progress of science and the arts, but the results belie their words. There is quite simply a mismatch between principle and results here: it is as if the honorable and well-intentioned judges do not realize that the recognition of Constitutional principles has a definite cost–and that cost either has to be borne by the copyright owner or the public. Much of the problem stems from the fact that the judges are asking the wrong questions when they apply the statutory test. There is no such thing as a use or a reproduction which has no commercial *effect*, because the copyright owner will always "lose" notional revenue when a use or reproduction is made without payment. The question under the fourth factor should therefore not be: Is there market harm? Rather, we should ask *how much* market harm should the copyright owner bear, and *for what purposes* must she bear it? The question under the first factor also requires modification. It should not be: Is the work so transformative that it fulfills a different market purpose or function? Instead, we should ask what public purposes are fulfilled by the use in question. The degree of transformation should be accounted for under the "amount taken" test in § 107(3). We should still ask whether the use is commercial or non-commercial under § 107(1), but this question should illuminate the purpose of the use, rather than the market effect of the use.

In an ideal world, however, I would require even more of the judiciary than a simple reinterpretation of the § 107 test. In order to ensure that the market harm/market failure rhetoric never again dominates the judicial discourse, I recommend the adoption of a rebuttable presumption of fairness for the uses listed in the main body of § 107: criticism, comment, news reporting, teaching (and I would go so far as to include multiple copies for classroom use under this heading), scholarship and research.[58] This presumption could be rebutted by the copyright owner with evidence that the use is nothing more than disguised commercial free-riding, or that the use has a market destructive effect on the value of his copyright. Uses which are not specifically listed in the main body of § 107 could be subject to the general "no presumption" rule set out in *Campbell*, and the defendant would have the burden of proving the applicability of the defense in these cases. Although this proposal would result in the burden of proof being carried by the plaintiff in the majority of fair use defense claims, I think that the uncertainties of the market harm determination should inure to the benefit of the defendant when her infringement serves the Constitutional purposes of the Copyright Act.[59]

Although the cooperation of the judiciary is required for a fundamental rediscovery of the fair use doctrine, this would be a vain effort if private contracts were allowed to routinely disclaim fair use. I therefore endorse the proposal set out in H.R. 3048, which would add the following text to § 301 of the Copyright Act: "When a work is distributed to the public subject to non-negotiable license terms, such terms shall not be enforceable under the common law or statutes of any state to the extent that they: (1) limit the reproduction, adaptation, distribution, performance, or display, by means of transmission or otherwise, of material that is uncopyrightable under section 102(b) or otherwise; or (2) abrogate or restrict the limitations on exclusive rights specified in sections 107 through 114 and sections 117 and 118 of this title."[60] The elegance of this proposal is that it solves a variety of contractual problems from within the Act itself. Furthermore, it leaves room for negotiated contracts to disclaim fair use, thus respecting true expressions of contractual will. In addition, it effectively and clearly neutralizes the danger that UCC2B will facilitate contractual displacement of fair use.

H.R. 3048 contains another proposal which I think is essential for the continued viability of the fair use defense: it suggests an addition to the text of § 107 which would plainly state that the availability of the fair use defense is not affected by either the circumvention of a technological protection system, or by the fact that a work is transmitted in digital form by the copyright owner. Both of these statements are needed to ensure that fair use rights exist in the digital, as well as the hard-copy, realm. I would, however, go one step further than H.R. 3048 and include a statement within § 107 to make it clear that fair use is not affected by the removal of copyright management information.

EXPECTATIONS OF A EULOGY, HOPES FOR A TELEGRAM

The Constitution mandates that we balance the author's incentive to create with the public's interest in social progress. Authorship promotes social progress, but so does learning and scholarship: the Copyright Act should therefore protect all of them. If applied in its "public purpose" rather than its "market-centric" form, fair use could play a crucial role in balancing the rights of users and creators in the digital age. Instead, developments both inside and outside of the courts have fair use proponents scrambling to look for the "roots" or "real meaning" of § 107, like desperate diviners looking for the true meaning of life. It is time we faced the issue head-on: What is the purpose of the fair use doctrine? Is it meant to put certain infringements beyond the grasp of copyright owners, for specified public purposes? Or, is its role much more narrow, forgiving only those infringements that create works which the copyright owner would not authorize (as in the case of parody or criticism) or could not authorize because of transaction costs? If fair use recognizes that copyrighted works are the basic tools of research, education, expression and scholarship, then these uses should not be burdened with the full cost of every non-commercial reproduction. A rediscovery of fair use also requires that we explicitly recognize that the Copyright Act protects and promotes authorship in two distinct ways: it ensures that creators reap the fruits of their labors, *and* it ensures that creators do not have so much control over their works that they burden learning, scholarship, and the future generation of authors and artists.

Unfortunately, I am not any less convinced of the viability of the fair use defense than when I started this discussion. I still think that the activities in both the courts and in Congress indicate that fair use is dead, both on and off the Internet. My sincere hope, however, is that I am proven wrong. My sincere hope is that fair use can one day send a telegram to the American public: "Rumors of my death are greatly exaggerated."[61]

NOTES

1. I use this term as a shorthand way of referring to the combined effect of the "market failure" rationale–which states that fair use should only operate when a bargain cannot be struck between the owner and user of a copyrighted work; and the "market harm" approach–which places paramount importance on the market harm prong of § 107. These two factors are conceptually distinct, but tend to work in concert to erode the fair use defense.

2. It should be noted that I refer here to the legal operation of the doctrine. In the future, people may be able to use works without compensating the copyright owner, but my contention is that such use will only occur when copyright owners do not enforce their legal right to stop the use. This is very different from such uses being legally exempt from a finding of infringement. Obviously, there will always be some users out there that refuse to comply with copyright law, and some copyright owners who fail to enforce their legal right on every occasion. This non-enforcement may be motivated by altruistic choice, indifference or enforcement costs. The crucial thing, however, is that the right exists, and so the decision to enforce may be made at any

time during the life of the legal right. "Legal because you can't/don't want to/are too busy to catch me" does not fair use make.

3. Of course, I do not think that these required steps, nor anything remotely resembling them, will be taken by either Congress or the judiciary.

4. Art. I, § 8, Cl. 8.

5. Id.

6. 8 Pet. 591 (1834).

7. This is a highly simplified account of a complex body of theory that seeks to account for property entitlements. The natural right theory of property entitlements, for example, can be subdivided into "labor" and "personality" rationales. My truncated version is adequate for the discussion herein, however.

8. I have very consciously avoided phrasing these restrictions as "restrictions on use" because the copyright act does not grant a use right to the copyright owner. Unfortunately, it is difficult to avoid referring to the *effects* of the § 106 rights in terms of "use" because they do affect the user's ability to "use" works in specific, albeit narrowly defined, ways. For the sake of clarity, however, it is important to remember that the Copyright Act gives copyright owners the right to control certain specific "uses" of copyrighted works–such as the public performance of these works–but does not grant a general "use right."

9. Of course, I do not use "guarantee" in its absolute sense here. Not even the strongest copyright regime in the world can guarantee a monetary return to an author. What it can guarantee is that, if there is any money to be made, most of it will go to the copyright owner.

10. *Sony Corp. v. Universal City Studios, Inc.*, 464 U.S. 417 (1984) at 429.

11. Note, however, that this list is not exclusive, and courts can consider other public interest factors, such as the increased access to television broadcasts mentioned in *Sony*.

12. 17 U.S.C. § 107.

13. 471 U.S. 539 (1985).

14. Of course, these reasons are only "wrong" if you support a broad public purpose conception of fair use.

15. *Harper, supra* note 13 at 538.

16. *Campbell v. Acuff-Rose Music, Inc.*, 510 U.S. 569 (1994).

17. *Harper, supra* note 13, at footnote 9.

18. *Harper, supra* note 13 at 550.

19. See Judge Jacobs' dissent in *American Geophysical Union v. Texaco Inc.*, 60 F.3d 913 (2d Cir. 1995), *cert. denied*, 116 S. Ct. 592 (1995).

20. A fact which should not be taken too seriously, since there is support in the literature, the cases, and Congressional debates for every formulation, permutation and interpretation of virtually every section of the Copyright Act.

21. *Campbell, supra* note 16 at 592.

22. The principle of "aesthetic non-discrimination" was first enunciated in *Bleistein v. Donaldson Lithographing Co.*, 188 U.S. 239 (1903).

23. *Supra* note 10.

24. Boswell's Life of Johnson 19 (G. Hill ed. 1934).

25. *Campbell, supra* note 16 at 579.

26. Id.

27. 9 F. Cas. 342 (1841).

28. *Supra* note 27 at 348.

29. The *Campbell* case is no help in testing this supposition, since the case has not been pursued by the parties on remand.

30. 60 F.3d 913 (2d Cir. 1994).

31. This, of course, implies that the possibility of extra photocopies was already factored into the increased price of the journal subscription.

32. *Texaco, supra* note 29 at 930-31.

33. Id. at 930. Emphasis added.

34. In fact, some of the Court's apparent inconsistencies in tone máy have been the result of the fact that the judgement was amended twice, in response to an outcry from fair use advocates and copyright scholars. The fact that the Court's original judgement was much more hostile to fair use does not bode well for the future of the doctrine.

35. For more information on the technological possibilities, see Mark Stefik, *Shifting the Possible: How Trusted Systems and Digital Property Rights Challenge Us to Rethink Digital Publishing*, 12 Berkeley Tech. L. J. 137 (1997).

36. 99 F.3d 1381 (6th Cir. 1996), at 1387. Internal quotations omitted.

37. *MDS, supra* note 34 at 1385. Internal citations omitted.

38. *Supra* note 10.

39. This type of legal oversight regulates the *process* of contract formation. There is an independent ground of review, which operates from outside contract law itself, and which overturns contracts based on their *content*–even when they are formed properly. I will return to the regulation of the content of contracts when I discuss federal preemption later in this paper.

40. Of course, one of the main assertions in these software contracts is that the purchaser has licensed, rather than bought, the copy of the software. The distinction between a license and a sale is not important to our discussion, and can be truly mind-bending, so I will hold it in reserve for another day.

41. See, for example, *Step-Saver Data Sys. v. Wyse Technology*, 939 F.2d 91 (3d Cir. 1991) and *Foresight Resource Corp. v. Pfortmiller*, 719 F.Supp 1009 (D.Kan. 1989).

42. *ProCD, Inc. v. Zeidenberg*, 86 F.3d 1447 (7th Cir. 1996).

43. A principle resoundingly upheld in *Feist Publications v. Rural Telephone Services*, 499 U.S. 340 (1991).

44. In this regard it is interesting to note technological protection systems, accompanied by contractual admonitions of secrecy, could also be used to bring material traditionally protected by copyright under the protective umbrella of trade secret law.

45. Like all articles of the Uniform Commercial Code, UCC2B is being drafted by the National Conference of Commissioners on Uniform State Laws (NCCUSL) and the American Law Institute (ALI). And like all articles of the UCC, 2B will not become law until it is enacted by individual state legislatures.

46. It should be noted that H.R. 2281 includes the text of the controversial database legislation bill, H.R. 2652, which is included in Title V of the Act. The WIPO treaties specifically omitted the database protection provisions that were proposed by

the U.S. delegation in December of 1996, and so H.R. 2281 goes far beyond what is necessary to implement the WIPO copyright treaties. If enacted, the database provisions pose a separate threat to fair use because they protect facts–traditionally uncopyrightable material–and because they create an extraction right which is fundamentally at odds with the notion of fair use. Although the bill does include an educational use exception, see § 1303(d) of Title V, this exception only operates if it does not "harm directly the actual market for the product or service referred to in section 1302." Because a database makes money when it is used as a source of information, any use which: (a) seeks to make an uncompensated extraction from that database; or (b) provides a separate, competing, source for information lawfully extracted from a database, could harm the market for the database. Any published scholarly paper could act as a separate, competing source if it contains information originally extracted from a database. This exception may only operate when a database owner refuses to enforce her section 1302 rights, or when the data is not incorporated into any publicly available document.

47. See Title I, Sec. 103, 1201 (c) of H.R. 2281.

48. This observation may seem overly paranoid, but Representative Coble, for example, has suggested that the very presence of a technological protection system would affect the fair use determination.

49. This amendment was suggested by Commissioner Perlman.

50. See the Reporter's Notes to proposed Section 2B-110, in the most recent (August 1, 1998) draft. It can be found at: http://www.law.upenn.edu/bll/ulc/ucc2b/2b898.htm.

51. See *ProCD, supra* note 42.

52. *Basic Book, Inc. v. Kinko's Graphics Corporation*, 758 F.Supp. 1522 (1991).

53. Readers interested in a more knowledgeable account of the possibilities of technological enforcement of copyrights might want to read the following paper: Stefik, *supra* note 35.

54. See, for example, *National Car Rental System, Inc. v. Computer Associates International, Inc.*, 991 F.2d 426 (8th Cir. 1993).

55. *ProCD, supra* note 42. The Nimmer treatise shares this view.

56. A recent ruling granting a preliminary injunction in a click-through case stated only that there was a likelihood that the plaintiff had an enforceable contract, it did not rule that the click-through contract was actually valid as a matter of law: *Hotmail Corporation v. Van Money Pie Inc.* et al., C98-20064 (N.D. Cal., April 20, 1998).

57. *ProCD, supra* note 42.

58. And yes, I realize that this is quite a radical suggestion.

59. Obviously, I think that all of these uses serve to promote the progress of science and the arts.

60. H.R. 3048, section 7.

61. I have seen several variations of this quote, but all of them are attributed to Mark Twain. And yes, the message did appear on a telegram written by Twain himself.

Licensing Agreements: Contracts, the Eclipse of Copyright, and the Promise of Cooperation

Rob Richards

The simple days of copyright compliance have ended. Any library that wishes to provide access to electronic products must be prepared for massive change. From a selection decision through end-user training, electronic products require special consideration due to their license agreements, which are pervasive and unavoidable. They affect every aspect of the process.[1]

Liberty of contract is not an absolute concept . . . . It is relative to many conditions of time and place and circumstance. The Constitution has not ordained that the forms of business shall be cast in imperishable molds.[2]

Rob Richards is Technical Services Librarian, University of Colorado Law Library, Campus Box 402, Boulder, CO 80309.

The author wishes to thank Barbara A. Bintliff, Director of the University of Colorado Law Library; Georgia Briscoe, Associate Director of the University of Colorado Law Library; Ann Okerson, Associate University Librarian, Yale University; Sally Morris, Director of Copyright and Licensing, John Wiley & Sons Ltd.; Terry A. Cullen, Electronic Services Librarian, Seattle University Law Library; Tony Arthur, Associate Librarian, Customer Services, University of Melbourne Library; Rebecca L. Eisenberg; and Matthew Kavanagh, for their support of this work.

[Haworth co-indexing entry note]: "Licensing Agreements: Contracts, the Eclipse of Copyright, and the Promise of Cooperation." Richards, Rob. Co-published simultaneously in *The Acquisitions Librarian* (The Haworth Information Press, an imprint of The Haworth Press, Inc.) No. 26, 2001, pp. 89-107; and: *Publishing and the Law: Current Legal Issues* (ed: A. Bruce Strauch) The Haworth Information Press, an imprint of The Haworth Press, Inc., 2001, pp. 89-107. Single or multiple copies of this article are available for a fee from The Haworth Document Delivery Service [1-800-342-9678, 9:00 a.m. - 5:00 p.m. (EST). E-mail address: getinfo@haworthpressinc.com].

INTRODUCTION

Acquisitions librarians have always needed to develop expertise in certain areas of law, including copyright, purchasing, and record keeping. The proliferation of electronic resources has compelled acquisitions librarians to become skilled in yet another legal subject. Since nearly all electronic resources are licensed instead of sold, librarians today need a sure grasp of the principles of contract law as they pertain to access to digital materials.

This study will offer an account of the rise of licensing agreements in the library marketplace, and then discuss the principles and significance of licensing agreements for electronic resources. Finally, the paper will explore recent developments in several licensing projects: the drafting of Article 2B of the Uniform Commercial Code (U.C.C.); the LIBLICENSE initiative; licensing efforts in the UK, the European Union, and Australia; and the recent statement of principles by the International Coalition of Library Consortia.

THE RISE OF LICENSING AGREEMENTS IN THE LIBRARY MARKETPLACE

Licensing agreements are the means for "granting rights in property without transferring ownership of it."[3] As the Draft of Article 2B of the Uniform Commercial Code (U.C.C.) phrases the matter, "[a] 'license' is a contract . . . to use information, an information processing resource, or an informational property right."[4] The licensing agreements in which libraries are most interested grant rights to use intellectual property governed by copyright law. U.S. copyright law sets out five rights of the owner of a copyright: the rights to copy, prepare derivative works, distribute, publicly perform, and publicly display a copyrighted work.[5] Nimmer cites U.S. case law going back to the beginning of this century, referring to grants of less than complete rights in copyrights as "licenses."[6]

U.S. copyright law also grants rights to owners of a copy of a copyrighted work. These include the "fair use" provisions which facilitate scholarly research and communication, among them the right to make limited numbers of copies for scholarly purposes, and the right to quote limited amounts of material.[7] Further, the federal copyright statute provides to libraries the right to make archival copies of an unpublished work, to make copies for replacement of damaged or lost out-of-print works, and to make copies of articles and chapters for local users and interlibrary lending.[8] In addition to the language of the copyright statute, libraries have looked to directives such as the Guidelines on Multiple Copying for Classroom Use[9] and the Interlibrary Loan Guidelines created by the National Commission on New Technological Uses of Copyrighted Works (CONTU).[10]

Until quite recently, federal copyright statutes and the accompanying Guidelines served as the legal standard for use of information resources in libraries, since libraries owned the copies of the print and microform copyrighted works which filled their shelves. In the case of electronic resources, however, libraries in most cases no longer own the copies of the copyrighted works they make available. Instead, the rights of libraries and library users are governed by the terms of licensing agreements, which may or may not offer the licensee the same rights enjoyed under copyright law.

One way to gauge the growing importance of licensing agreements in libraries is to trace the mention of licenses in the library science literature. The author performed searches of Library Literature from the late 1970s to the present, to see how licenses and licensing agreements have been treated.

Before 1990, licensing is mentioned in the library literature primarily regarding access to microcomputer software[11] and commercial on-line services.[12] In 1988, Library Literature indexed two relevant works with the subject terms "licenses" or "licensing." In 1990, works begin to appear on licenses for CD-ROM products and tape-loaded databases.[13] In that year, Library Literature indexed 14 works with the subject terms "licenses" or "licensing." Starting in 1994, licensing is discussed in the context of remote access to electronic journals, as with the TULIP project, and access to other remote networked resources.[14] The following year, Library Literature indexed 18 works with the subject terms "licenses" or "licensing," and in 1997, 34 works.

The rapid shift to the development of electronic collections coincides with the appearance of discussions of the virtual collection, and a transition in collecting philosophy from "just in case" to "just in time."[15]

As electronic resources prove their usefulness to library patrons, as publishers grow more comfortable with releasing electronic products, and as librarians gain expertise in accessing digital titles, the electronic share of the library collection will continue to expand. In an increasingly digital acquisitions environment, licensing will likely surpass purchasing as the chief means for providing access to library resources.

THE SIGNIFICANCE OF LICENSING

A Contract Law Primer

Perhaps the most salient aspect of the transition from copyright to licensing is the change from working in an environment regulated principally via statute to one overseen by the terms of contracts. Individual contracts are ruled by the terms of contract law, as expressed in such works as the Restatement of Contracts 2d, and the Articles of the U.C.C. which treat contracts (principally Articles 2 & 9). While librarians need not master contract law in order, thoughtfully, to monitor licenses, knowledge of certain areas of contract law is very useful for the evaluation and negotiation of licensing agreements. Contract concepts which are especially helpful to librarians include the definition of contract, rules of formation, and the issue of standard form licenses.

First, contracts are promises between parties, which bind the parties to act or refrain from acting in particular ways.[16] The terms of contracts create rights and duties which are to some degree separate from the rights and duties that pertain in other areas of law.[17] Breaking a contractual promise renders the culpable party liable for damages and other penalties, and renders the wronged party eligible for remedies.[18] Contracts are enabled by state laws, nearly all of which are based on the Articles of the U.C.C. which treat contracts.[19]

Second, contract law determines what constitutes a valid–or "enforceable"–contract, and how valid contracts may be formed. In general, contract law requires that the terms of an enforceable contract express mutual assent of the parties–a "meeting of the minds."[20] Contracts are formed by the manifestation of an offer by one party, the acceptance of that offer by another party, and "consideration," or the condition of a bargained exchange between the two.[21] A party may express assent to an offer in words–either spoken or written–or by conduct.[22] If the receiving party disapproves of terms in the initial offer, she may in turn make a counter offer consisting of different terms.[23] This process of exchanging offers and counter offers may continue until the parties come to a mutual agreement of terms. In theory, all terms of a contract are negotiable. In most cases, this means that libraries may be able to renegotiate licenses which contain unfavorable terms.

One weighty issue complicates these matters for libraries, however: that of standard form licenses. Notwithstanding the notion that a valid contract should represent mutual assent of the parties, U.S. courts have recognized the validity of standard form contracts–or "adhesion contracts"–in which the licensee has no choice but to accept the terms of a boilerplate contract offered by a licensor.[24] In some cases, however, adhesion contracts have been judged invalid due to their divergence from the reasonable expectations of the weaker party, or due to their "unconscionable terms."[25]

In cases involving the validity of shrink-wrap licenses–the kind of standard form contract frequently encountered by libraries–court decisions have been mixed. Shrink-wrap licenses have been held unenforceable in several cases.[26] There is a recent trend to view shrink-wrap licenses as enforceable, however.[27] Moreover, the draft of the new U.C.C. Article which treats licensing agreements explicitly validates the terms of shrink-wrap and clickable form licenses–which it calls "mass market licenses"–as long as those terms are not unconscionable.[28] The new U.C.C. Article will be discussed further below.

Key Elements of Licensing Agreements

What are the particular aspects of a licensing agreement to which librarians should pay special attention? In a number of useful works[29] several authors have identified the following contract sections as especially important for librarians: definition of uses, users, and long-term access; licensor's obligation to perform; duration; warranties and liability; remedies, governing law and dispute resolution; security and usage monitoring; costs; service and support; and confidentiality.

Most licenses place severe restrictions on the use of the licensed resource, and dispense with fair use and reproduction rights guaranteed by copyright law. Okerson, Davis, and Buchanan recommend that librarians negotiate license terms to include fair use and copying rights equivalent to those provided by the copyright law, and that "users" be defined to include the full range of library patrons, including retired faculty and community visitors. Further, Okerson bids librarians insist on flexible means for providing long-term access to electronic resources, including "perpetual access to the years being licensed" or the provision of an archival format.[30]

Okerson, Stenlake, and Harper observe that in many license agreements, "licensors make no express representations concerning their obligations under the agreement other than the obligation to . . . 'provide licensee with access to the licensed materials.' "[31] The authors urge librarians to specify licensors' obigations in the contract. For CD-ROM or tape loaded materials, such obligations could include providing adequate search software and defect-free disks or tapes. In the case of access to remote online services, licensors' obligations could include taking specific steps to minimize service disruptions.[32]

Jensen and the LIBLICENSE team also encourage librarians to attend to the duration and renewal terms of licenses. As many licenses contain automatic renewal clauses, the authors recommend that every license contain dates specifying the duration of the contract, and that the licensor be obligated to give the library notice of an impending renewal or termination.[33]

Licenses frequently treat warranties, or assurances regarding the quality or capabilities of a product or service. U.C.C. Article 2, and the draft of the new Article 2B, provide for implied warranties as to the quality and "fitness" of acquired resources, the accuracy of information content, and the ability of components to function as a system, unless these implied warranties are explicitly waived in the terms of a particular contract.[34] As Jensen points out, most licenses explicitly disclaim any warranties not expressly provided for in the license.[35] Librarians must take heed to include desirable warranty language in licensing agreements. Licenses will also include terms absolving licensors of liability of various kinds. The LIBLICENSE team warn librarians to make sure that licensors remain liable for direct damages, and for damages "recoverable if the licensed materials are unavailable or there are errors or omissions from a database."[36]

Librarians should also provide for the possibility of a dispute arising during the duration of the license. The LIBLICENSE team recommend that licenses provide for injunctive relief in the event of a breach. They also urge librarians to specify the governing law of a jurisdiction that will be favorable to the library, and to identify an accessible location for dispute resolution.[37]

Davis and Norman Desmarais direct librarians' attention to licensing terms that oblige libraries to monitor usage of a resource, and even to regularly report usage data to the vendor.[38] Okerson calls for security provisions, such as authentication by IP address, that are suited to the needs of libraries with large and geographically distributed user groups.[39]

Determination of costs in a licensing arrangement can be extremely complex. Brennan, Hersey, and Harper advocate considering cost variables such as the number and location of sites accessing the electronic resource, the acquisition of multiple formats of a resource, and the definition of the user group.[40] The LIBLICENSE team state that pricing terms should be expressed clearly in the contract, that clauses should prevent the licensor from unilaterally altering pricing, and that terms should provide for price renegotiation some time before the renewal date.[41]

Davis notes that librarians must ensure that terms specifying the provision of services and products–such as "training, user support, product updates, and replacement discs"–be included in licenses.[42] Most licenses relieve licensors from providing such services unless specifically instructed in the license.

Many licenses also contain clauses preventing libraries from sharing information about the terms of the license with other libraries. The LIBLICENSE team provides sample contract language that permits libraries to disclose all but very sensitive license terms with other institutions.[43]

Waiver of Copyright Rights: The Perils of Licensing

All of the commentators cited above warn of the risk of relinquishing rights guaranteed by copyright when libraries enter into licensing agreements. What is the relationship, then, between the terms of a licensing agreement and federal copyright law, when the contract gives to the licensee fewer rights than those granted under copyright? Are such contract terms preempted by copyright law?

The answer as it appears today from case law and treatises is murky, but the general trend of thinking asserts that contracts in which licensees waive their rights under copyright law are enforceable. These arguments, articulated most clearly by the U.S. Court of Appeals for the 7th Circuit and by Professor Raymond Nimmer in Information Law and in the text of U.C.C. Draft Article 2B, privilege the notion of freedom of contract over the sovereignty of federal statutory law.

As Nimmer expresses his views on the issue, "[p]reemption claims are generally rejected in context of properly pleaded claims related to contract . . . The state interest in enforcing relational obligations provides an 'extra element' that avoids preemption unless the claim conflicts with the specific rules in copyright law."[44] Citing the decision of the U.S. Court of Appeals for the 7th Circuit in ProCD, Inc. v. Zeidenberg,[45] Nimmer notes the court held "that a contract and its enforcement do not create rights equivalent to copyright for preemption analysis. The rights involved are entirely different."[46] Nimmer grants that "copyright preempts some claims allegedly grounded in contract law" such as the right to copy a work, and that "copyright also preempts contract claims if the claim conflicts with an express copyright rule." It is often uncertain, however, "whether an express copyright rule precludes modification by contract. In most situations, an agreement may alter the effect of property rights created under copyright . . . A contractual waiver or modification of rights creates no conflict with copyright."[47]

Similarly, Nimmer's *Reporter's Notes* to U.C.C. Draft Article 2B declare the superiority of contract law over copyright, and assert the neutrality of Article 2B on the issue of preemption. "In determining when such preclusive policies [as preemption] apply," Nimmer writes, "courts accept that contract law generally prevails, but ask whether a particular contract clause in a particular setting conflicts with federal policies when balanced against the general role of contracts in the economic and legal system. How far the federal policies reach is uncertain in many respects. Article 2B approaches the issue from a posture of aggressive neutrality. As with contract law today, Article 2B sets out underlying contract law principles and leaves federal policy determinations to federal courts and federal law."[48]

As to the scope of fair use rights for digital works, Nimmer claims that "[t]hese are questions of federal policy. They must be resolved by courts and Congress, rather than state legislation."[49] In other words, copyright law and contract law are held to be largely autonomous realms, each creating and enforcing distinct powers and duties. As licensees of contracts to use electronic resources, libraries can become parties to agreements in which they waive some or all of their fair use and copying rights under copyright law, and such contracts will be considered valid, unless Congress or the federal courts declare otherwise.

With negotiated licenses, in which terms are altered until both parties come to a "meeting of the minds," libraries will have to insist on terms which create fair use and reproduction rights similar to those provided by copyright law. Yet shrink-wrap and clickable licenses simply dictate terms to licensees, who must either accept the terms as they are, or refuse the offer of contract, and thus the opportunity to use the electronic resource. Mary Brandt Jensen notes, however, that a standard form license can be considered merely an "offer" of terms to the library, to which the library has "the right to make a counter offer containing the terms under which they are willing to acquire" the resource.[50] Librarians can attempt to engage vendors in negotiations even over standard form contracts, and thereby obtain favorable terms for their users.

Whither Standardization?

Libraries consistently seek standardization, in order to facilitate efficient processing of resources and provide effective service. Libraries' support of federal copyright statutes was no doubt part of an effort to standardize legal conditions and procedures for intellectual property use, so that libraries could provide efficient access to resources. In the emerging realm of licensing divorced from copyright rights, libraries seem to have lost a valuable framework of legal standards. Recreating comparable fair use standards in the licensing environment appears particularly challenging. Librarians face formidable obstacles in the development of model licenses, such the variety of actual licensing scenarios, and antitrust laws that limit the degree to which publishers and vendors can cooperate with libraries to create standard contracts.[51] Yet some efforts at licensing standardization seem promising. A discussion of several of these initiatives follows.

CURRENT DEVELOPMENTS IN LICENSING

Drafting of U.C.C. Article 2B

Like other contracts, licenses for electronic information resources are enabled by state statutes. Most state laws which have heretofore regulated contracts have been based upon U.C.C. Article 2, which governs the sale of goods–that is, tangible property. The terms of U.C.C. Article 2 do not precisely fit the transactions facilitated by licenses for information resources, however.[52] As Nimmer explains, "The differences are manifested in both the conditional nature of the transaction [i.e., licenses are not sales] and that the value lies not in the goods, but in information and rights severable from the goods [i.e., the information and rights to use it that are the subject of licensing agreements constitute *intangible* property]."[53]

Therefore, in the late 1980s, a study committee of the American Bar Association proposed a uniform law for software contracts. By 1991, the National Conference of Commissioners on Uniform State Laws (NCCUSL), which cooperates with the American Law Institute (ALI) in developing uniform state laws, had "initiated a project to consider . . . a Uniform Software Contract Law."[54] After the software industry initially objected to a separate U.C.C. Article for licenses, several more study groups and committees were appointed to address their complaints. Finally, in 1995 the NCCUSL appointed a committee, with Professor Raymond T. Nimmer as Reporter, to draft a new U.C.C. Article to cover licensing agreements for information resources.[55] The Drafting Committee has thus far issued more than a dozen drafts, and solicited comment from representatives of industry, consumer groups, and libraries.[56]

Several commentators have identified substantial problems with Article 2B, particularly for consumers. These include the validation of shrink-wrap licenses, the ability of licensors "to escape the obligation to exercise reasonable care to attempt to exclude viruses when software is delivered over the Internet," the ability of licensors to eliminate their "responsibility for incidental and consequential damages," and the ability of licensors to repossess software from a licensee's computer.[57] In addition, some object to draft language that lets licensors decide "what law will govern their sales and where customers can sue them."[58]

In an analysis of U.C.C. Article 2B, Robert Oakley, American Association of Law Libraries' Washington Affairs Representative, identifies several aspects of the proposed law which bode ill for libraries.[59]

First, Oakley voices concern about the scope of Article 2B: section 103 asserts that the uniform law "applies to licenses and software contracts."[60] The Reporter's Notes to this section state that the Article applies, in addition to software, online, and Internet licenses, to "transactions involving licenses of data, texts and related information."[61] Though the original task of the Drafting Committee was to develop contract law pertaining to software resources, Oakley notes that Article 2B could potentially cover licenses for printed and microform products.[62] Moreover, Article 2B would cover licenses for databases, which currently do not enjoy copyright protection.[63] Libraries should be concerned that Article 2B could enable publishers and vendors to circumvent copyright law by licensing non-electronic products, as well as electronic resources, and to restrict usage of databases.

Second, as discussed earlier, Article 2B is neutral on the issue of the validity of contract terms that are inconsistent with federal copyright law.[64] In the absence of legislation or court rulings that explicitly hold that copyright rights preempt the terms of contracts, libraries will have to scrutinize each of their licensing agreements, and negotiate terms to ensure fair use and reproduction rights.

Third, Article 2B endorses standard form contracts–which it calls mass market licenses–including shrink-wrap licenses and clickable licenses.[65] In the case of these form licenses, Oakley argues that "when licensees give up rights granted to them under the Copyright Act, at the very least it should be called to their attention that that is what they are doing, and they should have to separately indicate their agreement to such a term."[66] Yet the latest draft of Article 2B does not specify that terms which limit licensees' rights under copyright law must be called to licensees' attention for separate assent. Libraries must therefore carefully parse the lines of standard form contracts to learn precisely what rights are afforded them. Though libraries will sometimes have no choice but to accept the terms offered by standard form licenses, assertive librarians may often succeed in renegotiating objectionable terms of such licenses.

Fourth, Article 2B allows the restriction of transfer rights, and thus validates contracts that override the "first sale" doctrine of copyright law. As codified in section 109(a) of the federal copyright statute, this doctrine grants the owner of a copy of a copyrighted work the right to sell or lend the copy without permission from the copyright owner.[67] A subsequent clause of the copyright statute permits nonprofit libraries to lend copies of software and phonorecords.[68] Section 502 of the April 1998 draft of U.C.C. Article 2B (section 503 in earlier drafts) appears to validate contract terms that negate "first sale": ". . . a term in a license restricting transfer of a contractual interest or of informational property rights is enforceable. A transfer made in breach of an enforceable term that prohibits transfer is ineffective."[69] This provision would seem to validate licenses in which libraries are prohibited from selling or even lending copies of a licensed resource.

The final version of Article 2B was scheduled to be approved by ALI and the NCCUSL in the summer of 1998, so that the uniform law could be submitted to state legislatures for approval in the fall of 1998. ALI leaders have voiced reservations about the latest draft of Article 2B, however. Citing concerns about the scope of the April 15 draft–particularly its coverage of information resources beyond software products, and its treatment of electronic contracting–as well as "technical problems," the deputy director of ALI announced on April 22, 1998 that ALI would delay final approval of Article 2B until 1999.[70] Further, Professor Charles R. McManis, leader of an unsuccessful attempt in 1997 to include copyright preemption language in Article 2B, may try again to introduce language that preserves in the licensing realm fair use and other rights granted under copyright law.[71] Article 2B may well undergo further revisions favorable to libraries before being submitted to the states for adoption, probably in 1999.

LIBLICENSE

In 1996, the Commission on Preservation and Access and the Council on Library Resources agreed to fund an initiative to organize resources that would be useful to libraries in the licensing of electronic resources. The LIBLICENSE project, with Ann Okerson of Yale University Libraries as Principal Investigator, and consulting assistance from Rod Stenlake of Yale University and Georgia Harper of the University of Texas System, now has three components: (1) an Internet discussion list, LIBLICENSE-L, (2) the LIBLICENSE World Wide Web (WWW) site, and (3) LIBLICENSE software.

The LIBLICENSE-L listserv < *liblicense-l@lists.yale.edu* > is an international Internet discussion forum that treats both general and particular issues regarding licensing agreements for libraries. Topics range from news about model licensing projects in various regions, to the terms of particular licenses. Representatives from publishers and vendors, as well as librarians, participate. Subscription information and archives may be found on the LIBLICENSE WWW site at *http://www.library.yale.edu/~llicense/index.shtml.*

In addition to providing subscription and archival access to LIBLI-CENSE-L, the LIBLICENSE WWW site < *http://www.library.yale. edu/~llicense/index.shtml* > offers several resources of use to librarians who examine and negotiate licenses. A "Licensing Vocabulary" is a glossary of terms often found in licensing agreements. Perhaps the most valuable section of the site is "Licensing Terms & Descriptions," which analyzes each component of a licensing agreement, explains its significance for library licensees, and offers sample contract language favorable to libraries. Topics covered include general clauses, such as those dealing with assignment and severability; authorized uses; licensors' obligations; warranties and liability; remedies, governing law and dispute resolution; and costs. The site features links to the full text of actual licensing agreements provided by publishers and vendors, and to other licensing related Internet sites. Moreover, LIBLICENSE provides a lengthy bibliography on published research into licensing.

To further assist librarians in crafting favorable licenses, and to contribute to the development of a model licensing agreement, the LIBLICENSE team has created a licensing software product. This resource, now in Beta test phase, reproduces the entire LIBLICENSE website in downloadable form, and offers a program that allows librarians to create a new licensing agreement with favorable terms, or to revise an existing license. The software guides the user through 18 sections of a model license, explains the significance of each section, and presents sample language for the user to copy and paste into a document. The software could be available to libraries by the end of 1998.

European Bureau of Library, Information and Documentation Associations (EBLIDA) and ECUP

Action is underway in the European Union (EU) to create uniform copyright legislation–termed the Copyright Directive–to cover all member countries. In its draft form, the Copyright Directive would severely restrict the use of electronic resources in libraries. EBLIDA, the association of national library organizations in Europe, has worked since 1994 to develop the European Copyright User Platform (ECUP), a project to advocate for libraries in the drafting of the Copyright

Directive and other intellectual property matters. Among the goals of ECUP is the creation of "model clauses for licenses for the use of electronic information," through negotiations among libraries, archives, publishers, and vendors.[72]

Like LIBLICENSE, ECUP has spawned several useful resources. These include an Internet discussion list, ECUP-LIST < *ecup-list@ kaapeli.fi* >; a WWW site < *http://www.kaapeli.fi/~eblida/ecup/* > featuring documentation and current information about the Copyright Directive and licensing matters, with links to actual licenses and to other licensing resources; and an effort at developing model licenses. The "Licensing Issues" section of the ECUP WWW site < *http://www. kaapeli.fi/~eblida/ecup/licensing/* > features the text of four model licenses, tailored to the needs of four types of libraries: national, university, public, and corporate. EBLIDA may cooperate with the LIBLICENSE team to seek further progress in the coming year.[73]

UK and Australian Developments

In the United Kingdom, a Working Party on Licensing composed of representatives from the Publishers' Association (PA) and the Joint Information Systems Committee (JISC), a higher education consortium, has made great strides in standardizing licenses. As Sally Morris of John Wiley & Sons explains, in July of 1997 the Working Party completed work on a "Draft Model Licence"[74] which provides "an extremely exhaustive list of definitions" and "a variety of alternative clauses for different situations and preferences."[75] This model license contains acceptable contract terms with which to address most licensing issues confronted by libraries and vendors.

In the coming year the Working Party hopes to issue three additional resources. First, a "Heads of Agreement" document will provide a standard outline for licenses, including "baseline terms"–or definitional "starting points"–for contractual concepts such as "site" and "archival rights." Second, the Working Party hopes to complete "three or four working model licences for common situations," such as electronic journal subscriptions and CD-ROM network licensing. Third, the Working Party plans to issue a list of standard definitions of terms, to which license agreements can refer.[76]

In Australia, the CAVAL (Cooperative Action by Victorian Academic Libraries) Consortium's Task Force on Library Licenses and Electronic Databases has issued a statement of licensing principles.[77]

The principles treat such issues as definitions of use and users, retention rights, "fair dealing" (the Commonwealth equivalent of fair use), governing laws, and pricing. CAVAL has already had success in using the principles to renegotiate licenses with small vendors, and hopes to employ the principles in talks with major vendors in the coming months.[78]

International Coalition of Library Consortia (ICOLC)

In March 1998, the ICOLC, formerly the Consortium of Consortia, an international group of 60 library consortia, issued a statement of preferred practices for licensing electronic resources.[79] The statement calls for vendors to accept licensing arrangements with consortia,[80] and to offer reasonable and flexible pricing arrangements for electronic resources.[81] In addition, the Coalition urges vendors and libraries to preserve fair use in the terms of licensing agreements.[82] To facilitate long-term access to electronic resources, the ICOLC bids vendors grant libraries a perpetual, transferable license "when the consortium purchases the content," as well as the right to make archival copies of licensed resources.[83] Further, the ICOLC insists on the right to share with other institutions usage information and other management data about licensed resources.[84]

CONCLUSION

For U.S. libraries, the rise of licensing as the means to access electronic resources often involves the negation of fair use and other rights granted by federal copyright law. In the absence of federal legislation or court rulings asserting the preemption of contract terms by copyright law, libraries will have to scrutinize each license to which they wish to agree, and negotiate terms to include fair use and reproduction rights. Increasing use of standard form licenses under U.C.C. Article 2B may limit libraries' opportunities to negotiate favorable contract terms. Among heartening developments for libraries, projects such as LIBLICENSE in the U.S, ECUP in the EU, the JISC/PA Working Party on Licensing in the UK, and CAVAL in Australia, have made great strides toward standardizing licenses. These efforts have resulted in agreements on standard definitions of terms, the development of model licenses containing terms that are favorable to libraries, and the creation of tools for authoring and revising licenses to ensure adequate use and reproduction rights. Though the licensing regime may eventually eclipse copyright, libraries are succeeding in employing a time-honored method–cooperation–to ensure access to information into the electronic future.

NOTES

1. Trisha L. Davis, *License Agreements in Lieu of Copyright: Are We Signing Away Our Rights?* 21 Library Acquisitions: Practice and Theory 19, at 27.

2. Benjamin Cardozo, Hartford Accident & Indemnity Co. v. N.O. Nelson Mfg. Co., 291 U.S. 352, 360-61 (1934).

3. Jay Dratler, Licensing of Intellectual Property § 1.01 (1994).

4. U.C.C. § 2B-103 reporter's note 2.a. (Tentative Draft Apr. 15, 1998).

5. See 17 U.S.C. §§ 106 (1)-(5).

6. The earliest case cited by Nimmer is Fraser v. Yack, 116 F. 285, 286 (7th Cir. 1902); Melville B. Nimmer & David Nimmer, Nimmer on Copyright § 10.01[A] (1997).

7. See 17 U.S.C. § 107.

8. See id. §§ 108 (a)-(e). For a historical treatment of fair use, see William F. Patry, The Fair Use Privilege in Copyright Law (2d ed. 1995). For a useful discussion of fair use for libraries, see Laura N. Gasaway and Sarah K. Wiant, Libraries and Copyright: A Guide to Copyright Law in the 1990s, 26 (1994).

9. H.R. Rep. No. 1476, 94th Cong., 2^d Sess. (1976), at 68, *reprinted in* Gasaway & Wiant *supra* note 9, at 231.

10. Conf. Rep. No. 1733, 94th Cong., 2d Sess. (1976) *reprinted in* Gasaway & Wiant *supra* note 9, at 237.

11. See for example Thomas L. Warrick, *Legal Aspects of Purchasing Microcomputer Software,* ASIS Bulletin, Aug. 1984, at 9, 10.

12. For instance, see Jeffery K. Pemberton, *Online Interviews Harry Boyle on CAS's New License Policy,* Online, Mar. 1988, at 19-25.

13. Examples include CD-ROM Licensing and Copyright Issues for Libraries (Meta Nissley and Nancy Melin Nelson, eds., 1990); Mick O'Leary, *Local Online: The Genie Is Out of the Bottle,* Online, Jan. 1990, at 15; and Patricia E. Sabosik, *Electronic Subscriptions,* The Serials Librarian, v. 19, no. 3-4 1991, at 59.

14. See Katherine Willis, Ken Alexander & William A. Gosling, *TULIP–The University Licensing Program: Experiences at the University of Michigan,* Serials Rev., v. 20, no. 3 1994, at 39; Susan Smith DiMattia & Norman Oder, *OhioLINK Cuts $23 Million Deal with Elsevier for Journals,* Libr. J., June 15, 1997, at 12; Mark F. Kendall, *How We Did It: Resource Sharing and License Agreements; a Report,* 21 Libr. Acquisitions: Practice and Theory, 253.

15. See for example The Virtual Library: Visions and Realities (Laverna M. Saunders, ed., 1993); and Elizabeth Fuseler, *Providing Access to Journals–Just in Time or Just in Case?,* College & Research Libraries News, Mar. 1994, at 130.

16. Restatement (Second) of Contracts §§ 1 to 2 (1981).

17. Raymond T. Nimmer, Information Law § 2.14 [1] (1996).

18. Restatement (Second) of Contracts §§ 344-356 (1981).

19. John D. Calamari & Joseph M. Perillo, The Law of Contracts §§ 1-6 to 1-7 (3d ed. 1987).

20. Restatement (Second) of Contracts §§ 17 to 18 (1981).

21. Id. §§ 22 & 71.

22. Id. §§ 18 to 19.

23. Id. § 39.

24. See for example Lechmere Tire and Sales Co. v. Burwick, 277 N.E.2d 503 (Mass. 1972).

25. A fairly recent example is Graham v. Scissor-Tail, Inc., 623 P.2d 165 (Cal. 1981).

26. See, e.g., Step-Saver Data Systems, Inc. v. Wyse Technology, 939 F.2d 91 (3d Cir. 1991); Vault Corp. v. Quaid Software Ltd., 655 F. Supp. 750, 761 (E.D. La. 1987), *aff'd,* 847 F.2d 255 (5th Cir. 1988); Foresight Resources Corp. v. Pfortmiller, 719 F. Supp. 1006, 1010 (D. Kan. 1989).

27. Two recent decisions come from the 7th Circuit: ProCD, Inc. v. Zeidenberg, 86 F.3d 1447 (7th Cir. 1996), and Hill v. Gateway 2000, Inc., 105 F.3d 1147 (7th Cir. 1997).

28. U.C.C. § 2B-208(a)(1) (Tentative Draft Apr. 15, 1998).

29. See for instance Ann Okerson, *What Academic Libraries Need in Electronic Content Licenses, Presentation to the STM Library Relations Committee, STM Annual General Meeting, Oct. 1, 1996,* Serials Rev., Win. 1996, at 65; Mary Brandt Jensen, *CD-ROM Licenses: What's in the Fine or Nonexistent Print May Surprise You,* CD-ROM Professional, Mar. 1991, at 13; Davis *supra* note 2; Norman Desmarais, *Understanding Software License Agreements,* Against the Grain, Dec. 1996-Jan. 1997, at 44; Patricia Brennan, Karen Hersey & Georgia Harper, Licensing Electronic Resources: Strategic and Practical Considerations for Signing Electronic Information Delivery Agreements (1997); Nancy L. Buchanan, *Navigating the Electronic River: Electronic Product Licensing and Contracts,* The Serials Librarian, v. 30, no. 3/4 1997, at 171; Ann Okerson, Georgia Harper & Rod Stenlake, LIBLICENSE: Licensing Terms & Descriptions (visited May 12, 1998) < *http://www.library.yale.edu/~llicense/table.shtml* >; International Coalition of Library Consortia, Statement of Current Perspective and Preferred Practices for the Selection and Purchase of Electronic Information (Mar. 25, 1998) (visited May 11, 1998) < *http://www.library.yale.edu/consortia/statement.html* > [hereinafter ICOLC]. For further information on the legal dimensions of licenses, see Raymond T. Nimmer, The Law of Computer Technology (3d ed. 1997).

30. Okerson *supra* note 30, at 67, 69; Davis *supra* note 2, at 24-26; Buchanan *supra* note 30, at 174-77.

31. Ann Okerson, Georgia Harper & Rod Stenlake, LIBLICENSE: Performance Obligations of Licensors (visited May 12, 1998) < *http://www.library.yale.edu/~llicense/perfmgen.shtml* >.

32. Id.

33. Jensen *supra* note 30, at 14; Ann Okerson, Georgia Harper & Rod Stenlake, LIBLICENSE: Term and Renewal (visited May 12, 1998) < *http://www.library.yale.edu/~llicense/termgen.shtml* >.

34. U.C.C. §§ 2-314 to 2-315, 2 U.L.A. 212, 380 (1989); U.C.C. §§ 2B-403 to 2B-405 (Tentative Draft Apr. 15, 1998).

35. Jensen *supra* note 30, at 14.

36. Ann Okerson, Georgia Harper & Rod Stenlake, LIBLICENSE: Warranties, Indemnities and Limitations of Liability (visited May 12, 1998) < *http://www.library. yale.edu/~llicense/warrcls.shtml* >.

37. Ann Okerson, Georgia Harper & Rod Stenlake, LIBLICENSE: Remedies; Governing Law; Dispute Resolution (visited May 12, 1998) < *http://www.library. yale.edu/~llicense/remcls.shtml* >.

38. Davis *supra* note 2, at 27; Desmarais *supra* note 30, at 45-46.

39. Okerson *supra* note 30, at 68.

40. Brennan, Hersey, & Harper *supra* note 30, at 8.

41. Ann Okerson, Georgia Harper & Rod Stenlake, LIBLICENSE: Payments, Fees and Costs (visited May 12, 1998) < *http://www.library.yale.edu/~llicense/paygen.shtml* >.

42. Davis *supra* note 2, at 24.

43. Ann Okerson, Georgia Harper & Rod Stenlake, LIBLICENSE: Confidentiality (visited May 12, 1998) < *http://www.library.yale.edu/~llicense/confgen.shtml* >.

44. Nimmer *supra* note 18 § 2.14.

45. ProCD, Inc. v. Zeidenberg, 86 F.3d 1447 (7th Cir. 1996).

46. Nimmer *supra* note 18 § 2.14[1].

47. Id.

48. U.C.C. § 2B-105 reporter's note 3. (Tentative Draft Apr. 15, 1998).

49. Id.

50. Jensen *supra* note 30, at 16.

51. Sally Morris, Copyright and Model Licences, Paper delivered to the Joint Information Systems Committee Strategy Conference, Manchester, UK (Apr. 30, 1998).

52. U.C.C. § 2-102, 1 U.L.A. 172 (1989).

53. U.C.C. § 2B preface pt. 1, at 5 (Tentative Draft Apr. 15, 1998).

54. Id.; David A. Rice, *Lessons About the Realities of Contract for U.C.C. Article 2 Revision and a Future Software Contract Statute,* 18 Rutgers Computer & Tech. L.J. 499, 499 n. 1 (1992).

55. U.C.C. § 2B preface pt. 1, at 5 (Tentative Draft Apr. 15, 1998).

56. Drafts issued since 1996 may be found on the NCCUSL web site < *http://www. law.upenn.edu/library/ulc/ulc.htm* >.

57. Gail Hillebrand, Consumers Union Comments on Draft of UCC Article 2B (Jul. 1997) (visited May 11, 1998) < *http://www.softwareindustry.org/issues/guide/docs/cun. html* >.

58. Cem Kaner, Article 2B is Fundamentally Unfair to Mass-Market Software Customers: Submitted to the American Law Institute for Its Article 2B Review (Oct. 1997) (visited May 11, 1998) < *http://www.badsoftware.com/ali.htm* >.

59. Robert L. Oakley, *Some Preliminary Comments on a New Issue for the Library Community,* AALL Spectrum, Feb. 1998, at 14 (visited May 12, 1998) < *http://www. aallnet.org/products/pub_sp9802.html* >. Oakley's comments refer to the Sep. 1997 draft. Of his objections to provisions of that draft, all but one still pertain to the latest draft of Apr. 1998.

60. Id. at 16; U.C.C. § 2B-103 (Tentative Draft Apr. 15, 1998).

61. U.C.C. § 2B-103 reporter's note 1. (Tentative Draft Apr. 15, 1998).

62. Oakley *supra* note 60, at 16.

63. Id.

64. Id. at 14.

65. U.C.C. §§ 2B-102 (30)-(31) (Tentative Draft Apr. 15, 1998).

66. Oakley *supra* note 60, at 15.

67. See 17 USC § 109 (a).

68. See 17 USC § 109 (b)(1)(A).

69. U.C.C. § 2B-502 (a) (Tentative Draft Apr. 15, 1998).

70. Jennifer B. Lucas, *Draft Uniform Licensing Law Hits Snag; ALI Will Delay Vote on Final Draft Until 1999,* 66 U.S. Law Week 2644 (1998).

71. Oakley *supra* note 60, at 14; U.C.C. § 2B-105 votes & action a.-b. (Tentative Draft Apr. 15, 1998)(visited May 12, 1998) < *http://www.law.upenn.edu/library/ulc/ ucc2/2b498.htm* >; Matthew Kavanaugh, *UCC 2B & Federal Preemption,* UC-CLAW-L, May 4, 1998 < *ucclaw-l@assocdir.wuacc.edu* >.

72. See ECUP-Info (visited May 11, 1998) < *http://www.kaapeli.fi/~eblida/ecup/ ecupinfo.html* >; and Dieke van Wijnen, *Libraries and Publishers Working Towards a Model Contract on Electronic Copying,* Against the Grain, Sep. 1995, at 71.

73. Ann Okerson, Personal communication to the author (Mar. 24, 1998).

74. Joint Information Systems Committee & Publishers' Association Working Party, Proposed 'Model Licence' Between UK Universities and Publishers (Jul. 1997) (visited May 11,1998) < *http://www.ukoln.ac.uk/services/elib/papers/pa/licence/intro.html* >.

75. Morris *supra* note 52.

76. Id.

77. CAVAL Task Force on Library Licenses and Electronic Databases, Statement of Principles Endorsed by CAVAL Council (Mar. 12, 1998); Tony Arthur, *Licensing in Australia,* LIBLICENSE-L, May 4, 1998 < *liblicense-l@lists.yale.edu* >.

78. Arthur *supra* note 78.

79. ICOLC *supra* note 30.

80. Id. § III.A.1.

81. Id. § III.B.1.-2.

82. Id. § III.D.1.a.

83. Id. § III.C.2.

84. Id. § III.D.2.

The West Copyright Conundrum

Ann Jennings

Many years ago, I had the opportunity to work on a product liability lawsuit against a major tire manufacturer. The case, involving an alleged defective tire which exploded causing the plaintiff to sustain severe brain damage, took nearly ten years to go to trial because the defendant pursued every remotely possible appealable issue prior to trial and exhausted every ostensible appeal after losing at trial, until the United States Supreme Court finally refused to hear the matter. My point in describing this case is that the tire manufacturer, who does undoubtedly make superior tires, refused to admit that it could make even *one* bad tire. And they paid 30 lawyers to defend their position. They would rather have spent millions of dollars defending their "honor" than helping an institutionalized man and his family. In the end, the plaintiff received the $1.2 million dollar jury award and an additional $300,000 accrued interest during the appeals (prior to paying attorney's fees).

In the world of legal publishing, there has been, until recently, really only one major publisher, West. In fact, prior to its purchase by Thom-

Ann Jennings is an independent law librarian, and co-owner and Director of Research of a research firm, InfoFacto: The Legal and Business Research Center, LLC, 145 King Street, Charleston, SC 29401. She also serves as Assistant to the Editor of *Against the Grain* and is the editor of a column on current issues in copyright litigation. Ms. Jennings recently completed a term on the American Association of Law Libraries Copyright Committee and she has coordinated several programs on the proposed Article 2B of The Uniform Commercial Code which addresses the licensing of information.

[Haworth co-indexing entry note]: "The West Copyright Conundrum." Jennings, Ann. Co-published simultaneously in *The Acquisitions Librarian* (The Haworth Information Press, an imprint of The Haworth Press, Inc.) No. 26, 2001, pp. 109-125; and: *Publishing and the Law: Current Legal Issues* (ed: A. Bruce Strauch) The Haworth Information Press, an imprint of The Haworth Press, Inc., 2001, pp. 109-125. Single or multiple copies of this article are available for a fee from The Haworth Document Delivery Service [1-800-342-9678, 9:00 a.m. - 5:00 p.m. (EST). E-mail address: getinfo@haworthpressinc.com].

son in 1997 and the subsequent divestments ordered by the Department of Justice, West had been strongly criticized for its monopoly on legal opinion publishing. The fact that the merger was allowed is a mystery to many. West Publishing (a.k.a. in library circles as the "Dark Tower") is just as protective of its ownership in copyright as the above-described tire manufacturer was of its product. And West has probably spent as much, if not more, money trying to prove this so. Way back in 1986, West successfully defended its claim against Mead Data Central, the former owner of Lexis-Nexis, when the Eighth Circuit ruled that "pagination was indeed an element of West's copyright" (see *West Pub. Co. v. Mead Data Cent., Inc.,* 799 F.2d 1219, certiorari denied 107 S.Ct. 962, 479 U.S. 1070, 93 L.Ed.2d 1010 (1986)). However, as they say in copyright circles, that ruling was handed down "BF" (before Feist) and this is "AF" (after Feist) and much has changed in the view of the courts regarding "sweat of the brow copyrights," particularly in the Supreme Court (*Information Law Alert* Feb. 11, 1994).

Feist v. Rural Telephone Service Co., 499 U.S. 340, 111 S.Ct. 1282, 1991 Copr.L.Dec. P 26,702, 121 P.U.R.4th 1, 18 U.S.P.Q.2d 1275, 18 Media L. Rep. 1889 (1991) removed copyright protection with regard to the selection, arrangement and coordination of facts in the white pages of telephone books and, in a unanimous opinion written by Justice Sandra Day O'Connor, rejected "sweat of the brow" while taking a more traditional view of copyright jurisprudence as an award for "creative expression, not hard work" (*Information Law Alert,* Feb. 11, 1994). In fact, in what was speculated to be an inferred rejection of the 8th Circuit finding in Mead, the Justice frequently referred to a law review article that was quite critical of the 8th Circuit decision in favor of West (see Patterson & Joyce, *Monopolizing the Law: The Scope of Copyright Protection for Law Reports and Statutory Compilations,* 36 UCLA L.Rev. 719, 763, n. 155 (1989)) (*Information Law Alert,* Feb. 11, 1994).

All of this brings us to the current matter at hand, *Matthew Bender & Company, Inc. and HyperLaw, Inc. v. West Publishing Company,* a suit which was originally filed in Federal Court in Manhattan (S.D.N.Y.) in February of 1994 seeking a declaration that West does not own the copyrights to the page numbers used in its reporters. Bender was later joined in its suit by the intervenor, HyperLaw, a small publisher of legal CD-ROMs. Both of the "plaintiff-publishers" sought to cross-reference the text of opinions published on their CD-ROM products with the West page and volume numbers, enabling users to provide the courts with the required citations. West, while admitting that it does not own the rights to the texts of the opinions it publishes, does claim copyright protection of the headnotes, key numbers, captions and page numbers (Wise, Jan. 29, 1997).

This article will review the cases and appeals before the 2nd Circuit and each party's interest therein together with the effect of the proposed "Database Bill," H.R. 2652.

THE BENDER CASE

As explained above, the purpose of the Bender suit was to obtain a declaration that "West does not hold a copyright on its page numbers or that use of the page numbers is protected by [the] 'fair use' doctrine of copyright law," 17 U.S.C. §107 (*Information Law Alert*, Feb. 11, 1994). In its complaint, Bender asserted that it had collected government published slip opinions and converted them into digital format using scanners. After retyping the documents, Bender wanted to reference the West page numbers only. It would not include any of the synopses, headnotes or other copyrighted materials (*Information Law Alert*, Feb. 11, 1994). The opinions without the West page numbers would lack commercial viability as they are the legal profession's "de facto standard for citation" (*Information Law Alert*, June 10, 1994). HyperLaw, Inc. subsequently filed a motion to intervene as it had an interest in the same issues being litigated by the plaintiff which was granted by the Court.

In November, 1994, West filed a motion to dismiss the Bender suit alleging there was no justicable controversy; i.e., that Bender had no cause of action against West because it would not be "under threat of litigation" by the defendant were Bender to bring a product to market. However, Bender's attorneys found the motion to be "disingenuous and without merit" citing West's vigorous defense of its copyrights to the page numbers as an "embodiment of the selection, arrangement and coordination of cases" in the past (*Information Law Alert*, June 10, 1994).

Surprisingly, West and Bender later entered into settlement negotiations in an attempt to amicably resolve the issue. Negotiations broke down in February of 1995 and the parties proceeded with discovery.

West then filed papers with the court maintaining that should Bender produce a CD-ROM using their page numbers, it would not sue for infringement (*Information Law Alert*, July 7, 1995). However, both Bender and HyperLaw preferred "judicial determination that their activities are not infringing or that West's copyright does not cover its page numbers" (*Information Law Alert*, Oct. 13, 1995).

On May 2, 1996, Judge John Martin of the United States District Court for the Southern District of New York ruled on West's Motions to Dismiss both Matthew Bender and HyperLaw (*Matthew Bender & Co., Inc. and Hyperlaw, Inc. v. West Publishing*, 1995 Copr.L.Dec. P 27,505, 24 Media L. Rep. 1972) and found there to be three issues to which a determination must be made: (1) Intent and Ability to Produce; (2) Reasonable Apprehension of Suit; and (3) Mootness. The last issue referred only to Bender and West's representation that it would not sue them with regard to the New York version of their CD-ROM product "or any future version of that product produced in the same manner." However, Bender later filed a supplemental complaint also seeking a declaration as the publisher was in the process of producing a second New York product substantially different from the first and the court determined that an actual controversy did exist and, therefore, denied West's motion to dismiss on that subject.

Judge Martin's findings regarding the remaining issues were:

As to Intent and Ability to Produce:

The Court found that Bender had met its burden "of showing by a preponderance of the evidence that it had the intention and ability to produce the New York product at the time it filed the complaint." Bender did this by providing affidavits verifying the retention of a management consultant to study the feasibility of a New York disc, requesting vendor bids, producing a beta product, and collecting thousands of opinions from the State of New York.

As to Reasonable Apprehension of Suit:

Bender produced evidence of two meetings with West in 1993 wherein the defendant told Bender that their database contained some "proprietary elements which West had protected in the past and which West would protect in the future." Further, West testified in deposition that it decided whether or not to sue "on a case-by-case basis after having the opportunity to examine a finished product." Bender did not have a product on the market prior to filing suit. Judge Martin agreed that Bender proved by a preponderance of the evidence that it had a reasonable apprehension of suit.

On the other hand, with regard to these two issues, HyperLaw, by and through its president, Alan Sugarman, stated that although "it has taken every preparatory step possible short of actual infringement," it would not add the West page numbers to its product unless and until the Court granted declaratory relief. Should this occur, HyperLaw alleged that it had the ability to insert the data to existing opinions quickly and without preparation. Also, HyperLaw asserted that it had contacted West on several occasions and had been threatened with litigation (*Matthew Bender & Co., Inc. and Hyperlaw, Inc. v. West Publishing*, 1995 Copr.L.Dec. P 27,505, 24 Media L. Rep. 1972 (1996)). West contested these factual allegations and after a separate evidentiary hearing held on June 21, 1996, the Court ruled that Hyper-Law had met its burden of proof with regard to both issues: that it intended and was able to add the controversial features and that the only thing that prohibited it from doing so was its "fear of being sued" (*Matthew Bender & Co., Inc. and Hyperlaw, Inc. v. West Publishing*, 24 Media L. Rep. 2342 (1996)).

In November, Judge Martin heard and ruled from the bench on the plaintiffs' Motions for Summary Judgment and found that West had "no copyright protection for the pagination system used in its case reporters" and that West used its claim of copyright protection "to create a monopoly over reported decisions." Ruling only as to Matthew Bender (he found that there were disputed issues of fact concerning HyperLaw), it was Martin's opinion that the pagination issue was controlled by the decision in *Feist v. Rural Telephone Service, Co.,* and stated that West's page numbering system does not "reflect its intellectual effort" but rather was an "accident of where a particular portion of an opinion ended up in a West reporter" (Wise, Nov. 29, 1996).

Martin went further and ruled that even if West's pagination system were protected, "Bender's use of star pagination would constitute fair use." Regarding the nature of the work and the amount taken, Judge Martin characterized West's work as a "compilation" and stated that "star pagination does not in any way take advantage of that part of West's effort in making the compilation that reflects its intellectual effort." Likewise, "star pagination does not take a substantial amount in relation to the copyrighted work as a whole. West has its copyright because of the compilation, not because of where a particular portion of court-authored text falls on a page."

Finally, as to the effect on the market, the Court found that this issue did not weigh in favor of West. Star pagination does not "impact on the market for those who want printed books in which they can look at the decisions . . . it simply will effect the market for text of the court decisions. But West has no copyright on the text of the court decision. It only has a copyright in compilation" (*BNA's Patent, Trademark & Copyright Journal* Nov. 28, 1996 and *Matthew Bender & Co., Inc. and Hyperlaw, Inc. v. West Publishing*, 41 U.S.P.Q. 1321 (1996)).

The opinion was referred to in *The National Law Journal* as "a shot heard 'round the legal publishing world." West later released a statement claiming that "three courts have found in favor of West's star pagination copyright claims–and one has not. There is a conflict that obviously needs to be resolved. West will appeal" (Leibowitz, Dec. 9, 1996).

THE HYPERLAW CASE

As stated above, HyperLaw joined the initial Matthew Bender claim as an intervenor-plaintiff in March of 1994. HyperLaw is an electronic legal publishing company formed in 1991 by Alan D. Sugarman. The company publishes over 39,000 United States Supreme Court and United States Court of Appeals opinions on CD-ROM at "prices not inflated by monopolistic practices and artificial barriers to information maintained by or acquiesced in by the courts and the other branches of government" (http://www.hyperlaw.com/index.htm). A small percentage of the cases were retrieved by scanner directly from West's electronic databases. HyperLaw wanted to "expand its database by copying from West's volumes any ruling that is cited in a post-1990 decision" and it designed software specifically for that purpose (Wise, May 21, 1997).

While Judge Martin had found in August, 1995 that HyperLaw had met its burden regarding justicability, he also found in November of 1996 that the HyperLaw claim raised factual questions separate from those raised by Matthew Bender, specifically whether "the alternative and parallel citations are really a substantial contribution that gives [West] a separate copyright" and he ordered HyperLaw and West to trial.

West described the parallel citations as editorial enhancements "which are creatively selected and compiled and arranged by attorney editors at West from among a myriad variety." The attorney for West agreed that it was "not the parallel citation text that is copyrightable. It is the selection and arrangement and coordination of the parallel citation in the case report" that protects its usage (*Matthew Bender & Co., Inc. and Hyperlaw, Inc. v. West Publishing*, 41 U.S.P.Q. 1321 (1996)). However, Judge Martin, in a ruling published on May 19, 1997, again found on behalf of the plaintiff and ruled that those changes were too "trivial" to warrant copyright protection. "West's compilation copyright protects its arrangement of cases, its indices, its headnotes and its selection of cases for publication, but these are not what HyperLaw is copying." Further, he said that HyperLaw copies what are basically government documents written by federal judges (*Matthew Bender & Co., Inc. and Hyperlaw, Inc. v. West Publishing*, 1997 Copr.L.Dec. P 27,638, 25 Media L.Rep. 1856 (1997)). Judge Martin opined that "West's case reporters were 'derivative' works, meaning they were an upgraded product based on government documents, which would otherwise be in the public domain. In order to assert protection for a derivative work . . . West had to show that the decisions, as reported in its volumes, reflect 'an original work' of authorship. Rather than rising to that level, he concluded that the editorial changes are mostly factual or reflect the mechanical application of pre-existing rules." Further, he found that while West " 'clearly expends considerable time and money' in correcting inaccurate citations and other errors in opinions. Nonetheless, . . . there is 'no element of creativity or originality involved in these corrections' " (Wise, May 21, 1997).

THE WEST CASE

The appeals filed by West in these cases perhaps best describe the issues propounded by the defendant-appellant. And, as evidence of its determination to protect its interests, West pulled out a "big gun" in its case against Bender and HyperLaw in the form of Harvard University Law School Professor Arthur R. Miller. Professor Miller argued that "a reversal was necessary to square the 1976 federal copyright law with the realities of modern computer technology." The main arguments put forth by West in its brief were:

Under all applicable standards, West's editorial enhancements are entitled to copyright protection. In support of its claim, West cited *Alfred Bell & Co. v. Catalda Fine Arts, Inc.*, 191 F.2d 99, 102-3 (2d Cir. 1951), which states:

> . . . [A] "copy of something in the public domain" will support a copyright if it is a "distinguishable variation" . . . All that is needed to satisfy both the Constitution and the statute is that the "author" contributed something more than a "merely trivial" variation, something recognizably "his own." Originality in this context "means little more than a prohibition of actual copying." No matter how poor artistically the author's addition, it is enough if it be his own.

The District Court erroneously denied copyright protection to hundreds of thousands of case reports based on its cursory analysis of what West does "in most instances."

The District Court's findings as to "originality" are contradicted by the record and contrary to law.

An amici curiae brief was filed on behalf of the appellees by the American Association of Law Libraries, the American Library Association, the Association of Research Libraries, the Medical Library Association, the Society of American Archivists and the Special Libraries Association which asserted that:

> [A]lthough the case specifically deals with access to federal court case law that is binding on United States citizens, the lower court's ruling also provides important precedent for no fee public access to other information published by the United States Government. Such information includes census data, Labor Department statistics and information (e.g., the Consumer Price Index, wage information, unemployment figures), Congressional information (e.g., text and status of legislation), trade statistics, regulatory information, and medical data . . . If West's position were sustained, it would "extend copyrightability to minuscule variations" to preexisting texts and "would simply put a weapon for harassment in the hands of mischievous copiers intent on appropriating and monopolizing public domain work." L. Batlin & Son, Inc. v. Snyder, 536 F.2d 486, 492 (2d Cir.)(en banc), cert. denied, 429 U.S. 857 (1976). Contrary to West's assertion . . . to afford copyright protection to West's editorial revisions to judi-

cial opinions would impede public access to government information . . . Moreover, the Libraries believe that adoption of West's position in this case would not only chill West's commercial competitors, but also would compromise the ability of noncommercial entities, like libraries, to place federal court decisions or portions thereof online without infringing West's alleged copyrights. Further, West's claims would set a dangerous precedent, *permitting a republisher of United States Government information to embellish it with trivial variations and a few snippets of obvious, commonplace facts–without giving the public any notice or indications of where those revisions have been made–and obtain a "stealth" copyright over the entire work* (emphasis added). This outcome would stifle no fee access to public domain works and wrongfully discourage their use. It would be contrary to the public interest and an anathema to the purposes of copyright law.

At oral argument, the two main issues addressed were star pagination and copyrighting the text of opinions, the latter of which only HyperLaw was an appellee. As to the issue of star pagination, Professor Miller cited technological advances and argued that "something 'much bigger than page numbers' was at stake. In cyberspace, he explained, there are no page numbers, only markers." It was his contention that ultimately the "markers" could be used to recreate relevant portions of any work, including his own treatise, *Federal Practice & Procedure*, without prohibited copying ever taking place. Competitors' use of the West page numbers was nothing less than "embedding on a CD-ROM West's 'entire template, its selection, coordination and arrangement.' "

This notion was sharply challenged by attorneys for both Matthew Bender and the U.S. Department of Justice which had been allowed five minutes of argument as an amicus curiae. Bender's lawyer, Morgan Chu, countered that "only a crazed lunatic would copy West's opinions in the order they are published in case reports." What was actually at stake was the ability to "pinpoint" citations. Further, he argued, that to assert that its citations cannot be used by rivals was "a stunning proposition and perversion of the copyright law."

In his address, Justice Department lawyer David Seidman told the court that because of the "speed and ease" with which lawyers can access opinions electronically, the "economic value of West's compilation [in its case reports] is not what it once was." Mr. Seidman warned that it was not the role of the courts "to protect against the consequences of technological change."

The second, and potentially more sweeping ruling, "that West has no protection for the text of individual opinions it publishes," was somewhat less heated. James Rittinger represented West on the text issue and as such he defended West's editorial changes, telling the panel that "there is no dispute that West's enhancements had surpassed the Supreme Court's 'modicum of originality' test." In parting, however, Mr. Rittinger accused HyperLaw of "reaping where [it has] not sown."

On behalf of HyperLaw, Carl Hartmann told the panel that his client was seeking to use nothing other than the "facts" in West's reporters. Those facts, he contended, "consisted of additions made by West such as attorneys' names or subsequent history, and the body of the court opinion itself, a government document" (Wise, Mar 17, 1998).

The oral arguments before the Second Circuit Court of Appeals were heard on March 16, 1998 and the Court's opinions were handed down on November 3, 1998, upholding the rulings which allowed Bender and Hyperlaw to produce CD-ROMs for use in legal research and to use West Publishing Co.'s star pagination location system for citing cases (WSJ, 11/05/98).The reasons were twofold as to why the Court rejected West's argument:

> Even if plaintiffs' CD-ROM discs (when equipped with star pagination) amounted to unlawful copies of West's arrangement of cases under the Copyright Act, (i) West has conceded that specification of the initial page of a West case reporter in plaintiffs' products ("parallel citation") is permissible under the fair use doctrine, (ii) West's arrangement may be perceived through parallel citation and thus the plaintiffs may lawfully create a copy of West's arrangement of cases, (iii) the incremental benefit of star pagination is that it allows the reader to perceive West's page breaks within each opinion, which are not protected by its copyright, and (iv) therefore star pagination does not create a "copy" of any protected elements of West's compilations or infringe West's copyrights.

In any event, under a proper reading of the Copyright Act, the insertion of star pagination does not amount to infringement of West's arrangement of cases (Docket No. 97-7430. ___ F3d ___, 1998 WL 764841 (1998))

In the second action, the Second Circuit ruled in favor of Hyperlaw, stating that while:

It is true that neither novelty nor invention is a requisite for copyright protection, but minimal creativity is required. Aside from its syllabi, headnotes and key numbers–none of which HyperLaw proposes to copy–West makes four different types of changes to judicial opinions that it claimed at trial are copyrightable: (i) rearrangement of information specifying the parties, court, and date of decision; (ii) addition of certain information concerning counsel; (iii) annotation to reflect subsequent procedural developments such as amendments and denials of rehearing; and (iv) editing of parallel and alternate citations to cases cited in the opinions in order to redact ephemeral and obscure citations and to add standard permanent citations (including West reporters). All of West's alterations to judicial opinions involve the addition and arrangement of facts, or the rearrangement of data already included in the opinions, and therefore any creativity in these elements of West's case reports lies in West's selection and arrangement of this information. In light of accepted legal conventions and other external constraining factors, West's choices on selection and arrangement can reasonably be viewed as obvious, typical, and lacking even minimal creativity. Therefore, we cannot conclude that the district court clearly erred in finding that those elements that HyperLaw seeks to copy from West's case reports are not copyrightable . . . (Docket No. 97-7910. ___ F3d ___, 1998 WL 764837 (1998))

According to an American Association of Law Libraries press release issued November 4, 1998, the findings follow "the recommendations raised by The American Association of Law Libraries (AALL) and five major library associations in their amicus brief filed in the first of these cases, which urged the court to uphold the important right of access to public information." Jim Heller, AALL President, stated that "this is an important victory for the access to government information, and in this particular situation, to judicial decisions. The American Association of Law Libraries believes that the public must have free access to state and federal court decisions, legislative, administrative regulations and other information that is produced by governmental agencies at taxpayers' expense" (AALL Press Release: Ruling on Amicus Brief, 11/04/98).

THE DATABASE BILL

This is the familiar title for what is actually H.R. 2652, the "Collections of Information Antipiracy Act," a bill introduced by Representative Howard Coble of North Carolina on October 9, 1997 for the purpose of preventing the misappropriation of collections of information. The bill would amend Title 17 of the U.S. Code (the Copyright Act of 1976) by adding a Chapter 12, the first section of which states:

> Any person who extracts, or uses in commerce, all or a substantial part, measured either quantitatively or qualitatively, of a collection of information gathered, organized, or maintained by another person through the investment of substantial monetary or other resources, so as to cause harm to the actual or potential market of that other person, or a successor in interest of that other person, for a product or service that incorporates that collection of information and is offered or intended to be offered for sale or otherwise in commerce by that other person, or a successor in interest of that person, shall be liable to that person or successor in interest for the remedies set forth in section 1206.

Depending on who you ask, the Database Bill is designed either "to provide much-needed copyright protection to databases and other 'sweat of the brow' compilations of facts or [is] an overly broad solution to a non-problem that will strangle academic and scientific research and permanently remove most collections of information from the public domain." Its intended purpose is to accomplish two goals: (1) to bring the United States into line with a European Union (EU) directive which requires member countries and their trading partners to adopt reciprocal *sui generis* database protection laws (a *sui generis* law is similar to copyright law in that it "gives database owners exclusive ownership of the information contained in those databases for specific periods of time"); and (2) to protect the publisher's financial investments from "free riders" who could "swipe their expensively and painstakingly gathered data and use it to compete against them."

In other words, the Database Bill would protect those databases not currently covered by the Copyright Act (as a result of *Feist*) by making it a federal violation to misappropriate such collections of information on which the owners have spent considerable time, effort and money albeit regardless of the level of originality or creativity the databases may involve. It would permit the use of individual items of information and other insubstantial parts; gathering or use of information through other means; the use of information for verification purposes; non-profit educational, scientific or research uses; the use of information news reporting; and/or the use of lawfully made copies of all or parts of a collection of information from selling or otherwise disposing of the possession of that copy.

The bill excludes from protection "collections of information gathered, organized or maintained by federal, state or local governments." It further excludes "computer programs used in the production or maintenance of databases, but not collections of information directly or indirectly incorporated in a computer program."

In the cases involving Matthew Bender & Co., Hyperlaw Inc. and West Publishing Co., Judge Martin ruled that West's copyright protects its arrangement of legal opinions, its indices, its headnotes and its selection of cases for publication, but not the opinions themselves, which are public documents, nor its book and page citation numbers. The Database Bill, if passed in its current form, would negate any such holdings by the courts. In testimony before the House Subcommittee on Courts and Intellectual Property, Hyperlaw President Alan D. Sugarman submitted a statement in which he charged that the proposed law is intended to protect the case reports of West Publishing and Lexis, the other giant in the legal publishing business.

Regardless of Sugarman's charge, "the bill is strongly favored by database publishing companies and their trade organizations while its provisions have raised major concerns for academics, scientists, journalists and librarians" who have actively lobbied against its passage. According to Paul Warren of Warren Publishing Inc., spokesman for the Coalition Against Database Piracy (CADP), "H.R. 2652 is about eliminating the inequity in a legal regime that allows an unscrupulous competitor to copy with impunity the contents of someone else's compilation and then destroy the first compiler's market by selling a competing, less expensive product." And, unfortunately, the government is said to generally favor the legislation "as a desirable first step toward balancing the public's access to information while protecting the incentives of database producers to collect and disseminate information" (Mayberry, Jan. 6, 1998).

The Database Bill was passed by the House on May 19, 1998 and was received in the Senate as S. 2291 the following day. The Senate Bill was sponsored by Senator Rod Grams, Republican of Minnesota. Minnesota is the home of West Publishing and many would say that it is no coincidence Sen. Grams sponsored this bill. In his speech introducing the bill, Grams asserted that the bill would allow:

> [D]atabase owners to receive adequate legal protection that provides them the incentives necessary to continue investing in database production . . . America produces and uses some 65 percent of the world's databases . . . These companies [database publishers] have been pioneers in offering innovative and easily accessible databases in any number of formats that meet consumer needs . . . despite technological innovations, creating and offering databases in the marketplace is neither cheap nor easy. Not only must database owners expend substantial resources on the collection of data, they must also maintain and distribute these information products, while continually updating them and responding to the demands of their customers.
>
> Many American jobs depend on a healthy, vibrant U.S. database industry. These companies employ thousands of editors, researchers, and others. They invest millions of dollars in hardware and software to manage these large masses of information.
>
> Despite the enormous value of these databases to our economy and society, American database owners are under a dual threat.
>
> On the one hand, after a 1991 Supreme Court decision [i.e., *Feist*], it is increasingly unclear whether most databases are adequately protected from piracy by U.S. copyright law.
>
> Lower courts since 1991 have handed down several decisions that have diminished the number and types of databases that are

protected under the compilation copyright provisions in the 1976 Copyright Act.

In addition, these decisions have stated that even if databases as a whole may qualify for this limited copyright protection, the facts contained in them are freely available for the taking and re-use by others–including competing database producers–without authorization or compensation. Although database producers do have means other than a new Federal law to seek protection, none has proven adequate, as is evidenced in the study completed by the U.S. Copyright Office last August . . . The European Union has begun implementing a new directive protecting databases in their own countries, but only those produced in the European Union or in countries that offer comparable protections. This law clearly is designed to disadvantage database owners not located in an EU country . . . As I mentioned previously, Mr. President, American database producers are anxious to continue producing valuable databases for worldwide use. However, the technologies present in today's world that allow for easy copying and redistribution of information threaten a producer's ability to continue receiving a fair return on the tremendous investments required to produce quality databases. Coupled with the inadequacy of U.S. law to protect investment in databases and the threat posed by the EU directive, it is clear to me that Congress–and more importantly, the Senate–must act quickly if we are to preserve the American lead in database production and use (http://thomas.loc.gov).

Grams' speech is quite disturbing when one considers that the rights of American citizens to public domain materials may be seriously compromised by this bill. Sen. Grams does not refer to those rights and he terms the Supreme Court decision in *Feist* "unclear."

In early October, 1998, both chambers of Congress approved the conference report (105-796) on the Digital Millennium Copyright Act (H.R. 2281) and on identical versions of the Copyright Term Extension Act (S. 505). President Clinton subsequently signed the bills on October 28, 1998 and they became Public Law No: 105-304. According to the American Library Association Washington Office Newsline (http://www.ala.org/washoff/alawon), "significantly, the H.R. 2281 conference committee deliberately elected not to include in its report the Collections of Information Antipiracy Act (S. 2291/H.R. 2652), a proposal to provide sweeping new legal protection for collections of information, including those not presently protected by copyright . . . While the legislative debate about how to implement the new WIPO copyright treaties and whether to add 20 years to the term of copyright protection may be over, both bills as finally adopted present ongoing opportunities and pitfalls for libraries, archives and educational institutions. Moreover, fierce legislative debate over database protection is expected to resume in earnest shortly after the new 106th Congress convenes in late January 1999."

WHAT NEXT?

According to an article published in the November 9, 1998 *Connecticut Law Tribune,* a spokesman for West in the Eagan, Minnesota office was quoted as saying the company is considering its appeal options. West's trial counselor, James F. Rittinger, of New York's Satterlee, Stephens, Burke & Burke, stated that "We could seek a rehearing en banc, or seek cert [i.e., certiorari or certification for the matter to be heard by the U.S. Supreme Court], and will definitely do one or the other. Thomson is going to continue to vigorously defend its intellectual property, with respect to wholesale copying." Further, Rittinger allowed, "This is a limited 2-1 decision in the 2nd Circuit, that relates only to the Supreme Court Reporter and Federal Reporter. West is going to continue to be diligent and aggressive, in the 2nd Circuit, using unfair competition or breach-of-licensing agreements." And, he said, "There's a reasonable chance that the database protection act will be passed in the next Congress. Win or lose, this doesn't have a financial impact on West."

We, of course, must take a wait and see attitude. Whatever the outcome, it's doubtful this fight will end anytime soon.

WORKS CITED

AALL Press Release: Ruling on Amicus Brief. AALL. Nov. 28, 1998.
Copyrights: Use of West law book page numbers in CD-ROM product is not infringing. BNA's Patent, Trademark & Copyright Journal. Nov. 28, 1996.
Leibowitz, Wendy R. *Matthew Bender wins a battle, but who'll win the case-cite war?* The National Law Journal. Dec. 9, 1996.

Library of Congress. http://thomas.loc.gov/bss/d105query.html. Sep. 11, 1998.

Matthew Bender takes on West Publishing's Copyright: Publishers battle over whether page numbers of law reporters are protected. Information Law Alert: A Voorhees Report. Feb. 11, 1994.

Mayberry, Jodine. *The database antipiracy act: Friend or foe of academic freedom?* Andrews Computer & Online Industry Litigation Reporter. Jan. 6, 1998.

New judge jumpstarts case: Will West dodge the copyright bullet? Information Law Alert: A Voorhees Report. Oct. 13, 1995.

Scheffey, Thomas. *West loses key copyright claims to U.S. Law.* Connecticut Law Tribune, Vol. 24, No. 45. Nov. 9, 1998.

Sugarman, Alan D. HyperLaw, Inc. http://www.hyperlaw.com/index.htm. Apr. 28, 1998.

Technology Briefs: West Publishing Loses Court Appeal. Wall Street Journal Interactive Version, http://interactive.wsj.com/edition/current/summaries/techmain.htm. Nov. 5, 1998.

Victory for Matthew Bender? Will West copyright claims on page numbering? Information Law Alert: A Voorhees Report. July 7, 1995.

West to Bender: You got no copyright case. Information Law Alert: A Voorhees Report. June 10, 1994.

WIPO Copyright Treaty and Term Extension Bills Clear Congress; Dangerous Database Bill Derailed But Bound to Return in 1999. ALAWON, Vol. 7, No. 125. American Library Association Washington Office Newsline, http://www.ala.org/washoff/alawon. October 13, 1998.

Wise, Daniel. *Legal publisher loses copyright on page system.* New York Law Journal. Nov. 29, 1996.

Wise, Daniel. *2D Circuit panel weighs West copyrights.* New York Law Journal. Mar. 17, 1998.

Wise, Daniel. *Some decision reports denied copyright protection.* New York Law Journal. May 21, 1997.

Wise, Daniel. *Trial airs case reporter copyright issues.* New York Law Journal. Jan. 29, 1997.

The Costs of the Loss of Copyright

Ron B. Thomson

Recent changes in copyright practice are posing a real threat to
scholars as well as to their publishers. The trend toward copying by
individuals, rather than purchasing their own original copies from the
publisher, has seriously hurt circulation of scholarly journals as well as
the sale of scholarly books. The effect of this is well-known: rapidly
rising journal prices as publishers try to recoup the basic publishing
costs from the sale of fewer and fewer copies. Copying under the "fair
use" doctrine has been extended in practice to nearly all areas of
scholarly research, without any understanding of the legislative limits
to "fair use." Scholars who copy, of course, think only of the immediate savings to themselves, rather than the over-all cost to the scholarly
community.

Now a second threat has arrived: the republication of published
scholarly work under the mis-belief that the so-called "Feist" decision
moves any "data" into the public domain. The threat here is more
serious since publishers will be unable to bring out original work of
certain types because there will be no chance to recover the editorial/
preparation costs of such work.

The type of work open to such abuse are scholarly critical editions
of ancient, medieval and early modern material, as well as such scholarly creations as catalogues raisonnés in the field of art. These works
are particularly costly to produce. All the editorial work, the typeset-
ting and marketing costs (to make researchers aware that these items

Ron B. Thomson is Director of Publications, Pontifical Institute of Mediaeval
Studies, Toronto, Canada.

[Haworth co-indexing entry note]: "The Costs of the Loss of Copyright." Thomson, Ron B. Co-published
simultaneously in *The Acquisitions Librarian* (The Haworth Information Press, an imprint of The Haworth
Press, Inc.) No. 26, 2001, pp. 127-129; and: *Publishing and the Law: Current Legal Issues* (ed: A. Bruce
Strauch) The Haworth Information Press, an imprint of The Haworth Press, Inc., 2001, pp. 127-129. Single
or multiple copies of this article are available for a fee from The Haworth Document Delivery Service
[1-800-342-9678, 9:00 a.m. - 5:00 p.m. (EST). E-mail address: getinfo@haworthpressinc.com].

127

now exist) are relatively high per unit sale, so that the sale of each copy of such books makes an important contribution to the overall enterprise. The actual manufacturing costs are relatively low; and so are the republication costs, whether the republication be of the entire edition, or simply the established base text without the supporting apparatuses.

The so-called "Feist" decision stems from an American court case between Feist Publications and the Rural Telephone Service Co. over the copyright to "white-pages" telephone directory information. The case was argued all the way to the United States Supreme Court [1991 111 SCt 1282 (decided 27 March 1991)] which decided in favour of Feist and allowed it access to the telephone directory information. There were really two issues which led to the court's decision. First there was a lack of originality in the selection and arrangement of the contents: all subscribers were included in the directory and alphabetical ordering was so natural that no creativity was involved. The court was not to be swayed by "sweat of the brow" arguments which had traditionally protected the work of the creators of data collections; originality and creativity were paramount. The second issue was that the company was required to make such a listing (a white-pages directory) as a condition of doing business; otherwise its customers could not access its service (connection to other subscribers).

What has happened is that republishers of data collections have taken the form of the Feist decision without its substance. There are actually very few data collections which lack all creativity in selection and structure; most involve some sort of selection by the creator and most involve some sort of imposed structure, both of which give the data base copyright protection.

In scholarly work, for instance in the preparation of a critical edition, the selection of the final form of the text (especially if it exists in multiple manuscripts as many medieval and early modern texts do) is a highly creative process, involving all the scholarly faculties of the editor. His familiarity with the language of the text, with the contents, with the predecessors, with the script, with the abbreviation systems, with the audience of the text, makes the selection of the final words very much his contribution. To argue as some have that this is just another data collection, is belied by the number of hours or years spent on the project. And certainly such an edition cannot be classified as a "condition of doing business."

But what has been the reaction to this by scholars? When this very issue was recently raised on a copyright bulletin board on the Internet, the general reaction was that loss of copyright protection was a "good thing" for scholarship. The scholar himself was rewarded with "career" advancement, "reputation" enhancements, and personal "self-satisfaction." For the publisher, however, none of these incentives apply. The initial publisher will find that the sale of his print run is sharply reduced as republication "guts" (or "creams") the market. Other scholars are quite happy to use simply the established text, knowing that "somewhere out there" someone has done the editorial work in a scholarly fashion; trusting the editor means that consulting the apparatuses is rarely necessary. Unlike periodicals, however, there is no "successive" market for scholarly publishers. Each book stands on its own, and is bought or not bought on its own merit. Losses on one item cannot be offset by raising the price of later items.

So the effect instead is that these texts will not be published at all or else published in a form which does not serve the scholarly community. Self-publishing is not really an alternative since the self-publication is not subject to peer review and the text is not vetted to the advantage of the user. Self-publications are also often poorly laid out, leading to confusion or wastes of time not associated with texts enhanced by the skill of an experienced scholarly publisher. Self-publications are also notoriously hard to obtain because there is no formal marketing, the title does not appear in normal industry listings, and the fulfillment centre is often difficult, if not impossible, to identify.

Similarly, electronic publishing has many disadvantages. The first is the malleability of the text, so that one copy may vary from another and there is no "set text" for the community to refer to. Reference itself is very awkward, so that a reader has difficulty tracking down a citation to a part of the text. And finally, with electronic storage systems becoming out of date within a decade or less, the accessibility of such texts is highly transient and the value of such work is reduced dramatically.

Copyright is easily circumvented by various mechanical means; the effect of the photocopier on scholarly journals is well-known. The response to the onslaught from the legal side on "data collections," however, will be different. The texts will simply not be available in the first place, and the losers will be the scholars who produce the texts as well as the scholars who hope to use them.

CONSTITUTIONAL ISSUES

Reno vs. ACLU:
The U.S. Supreme Court
Finds the Communications Decency Act
Unconstitutional

Steven P. Anderson

On June 26, 1997, in Reno v. ACLU,[1] the United States Supreme Court struck down the Communications Decency Act of 1996 ("CDA"),[2] regarded by many as the most sweeping piece of legislation designed specifically for the Internet. The CDA criminalized the knowing transmission by telecommunications device of "obscene or indecent" images or text to anyone under 18 years of age,[3] as well as the transmission to anyone under 18 of any comment or image that "depicts or describes, in terms patently offensive as measured by contemporary community standards, sexual or excretory activities or organs."[4]

Steven P. Anderson is Librarian at Gordon, Feinblatt, Rothman, Hoffberger & Hollander, LLC, 233 E. Redwood Street, Baltimore, MD 21202.

[Haworth co-indexing entry note]: "Reno vs. ACLU: The U.S. Supreme Court Finds the Communications Decency Act Unconstitutional." Anderson, Steven P. Co-published simultaneously in *The Acquisitions Librarian* (The Haworth Information Press, an imprint of The Haworth Press, Inc.) No. 26, 2001, pp. 131-143; and: *Publishing and the Law: Current Legal Issues* (ed: A. Bruce Strauch) The Haworth Information Press, an imprint of The Haworth Press, Inc., 2001, pp. 131-143. Single or multiple copies of this article are available for a fee from The Haworth Document Delivery Service [1-800-342-9678, 9:00 a.m. - 5:00 p.m. (EST). E-mail address: getinfo@haworthpressinc.com].

American jurisprudence has long classified "obscene" materials as undeserving of First Amendment protection. Therefore, the political and legal debate surrounding the CDA never dwelt on the lack of free speech protection for "obscene" material, but rather on the "indecent," "patently offensive," and sexually explicit communications just inside the scope of the legislation. Opponents of the CDA contended that the Act would outlaw web sites covering "safe sex" practices, medical and anatomy web sites, and even, as Justice Stevens wrote, "arguably the card catalogue of the Carnegie Library."[5]

Therefore, Reno v. ACLU is likely to be considered a landmark case for two reasons. First, it offers the latest constitutional analysis by the Supreme Court of the scope of First Amendment protection for various, non-obscene types of speech. Second, since it is the first Supreme Court case dealing with the World Wide Web, and the Internet in general, it will likely influence future legislation and court cases involving the newly networked world. This article will provide an overview of the Reno decision, followed by a commentary on the technological aspects and legal standards discussed in the opinion.

CASE BACKGROUND

The CDA was enacted as a small section of the much larger Telecommunication Act of 1996,[6] which dealt with much less emotional subjects, such as local telephone service and cable and over-air television broadcasting. The CDA provisions were either added in executive committee after hearings were completed or as floor amendments. After passage, Senator Leahy commented that the Senate, without any hearings whatsoever, "passed legislation overwhelmingly on a subject involving the Internet, legislation that could dramatically change–some would even say wreak havoc–on the Internet. The Senate went in willy-nilly, passed legislation, never once had a hearing, never once had a discussion other than an hour or so on the floor."[7] Congressional ambivalence notwithstanding, the President signed the CDA into law on February 8, 1996.

The new legislation was immediately challenged by the American Civil Liberties Union, and a host of additional plaintiffs, including the American Library Association, which were concerned over the breadth of censorship of non-obscene material on the Internet. The Federal District Court for the Eastern District of Pennsylvania assigned a three-judge panel to hear the case. The three judges, Chief Judge Sloviter, Judge Buckwalter, and Judge Dalzell, made 410 findings of fact regarding the use of the Internet and unanimously decided that the new statute abridged the freedom of speech granted by the First Amendment.[8] Under the CDA's judicial review provisions, the Supreme Court heard the case on appeal.

THE SUPREME COURT'S DISCUSSION OF THE SCOPE OF FIRST AMENDMENT PROTECTION

The Supreme Court examined several judicial precedents when deciding that the Act was unconstitutionally broad. In Ginsberg v. New York,[9] the Court had upheld the prohibition of the sale of indecent magazines to children under 17 years of age. However, the justices noted that the New York state statute in Ginsberg was much less restrictive than the CDA. For example, the New York statute did not prohibit children's parents from purchasing such material, as would have otherwise been restricted by the CDA. The Ginsberg statute applied only to commercial speech, a type of speech more akin to advertisement, which has traditionally been afforded less constitutional protection. By contrast, the CDA would have been applied to all forms of speech. Furthermore, the statute in question in Ginsberg extended only to indecent material which was "utterly without redeeming social importance to minors."[10] The CDA had no such restrictive definition; socially redeeming, though "patently offensive" or "indecent," material would otherwise have been illegal under the CDA. Lastly, the Court noted that the CDA applied to those under 18–not 17, as in the New York statute–thereby including an additional year for those nearest adulthood.

In FCC v. Pacifica Foundation,[11] the Supreme Court outlawed a vulgar and offensive broadcast which was not obscene on the grounds that it was relatively easy for children to tune into the afternoon radio broadcast. This decision was in keeping with other precedents which held that "each medium of expression . . . may present its own problems."[12] Therefore, because on-air broadcasting had a history of extensive government regulation due to the shortage of available frequencies on which to broadcast, broadcast speech could also be highly regulated. Additionally, broadcast material, by its very nature, could be highly invasive, potentially shocking the listener or viewer in their own living room.

However, the same factual issues are not present in cyberspace, the justices wrote in Reno. Internet access is not a scarce commodity, unlike radio and television frequencies which can carry only a set number of signals. In fact, quite the contrary is true, the Court observed: the Internet "provides relatively unlimited, low-cost capacity for communication of all kinds."[13]

In its analysis of the relationship between medium and speech, the Court examined Sable Communications of California, Inc. v. FCC.[14] There, the Court invalidated a blanket prohibition of indecent "dial-a-porn" telephone services. Unlike broadcast communications at issue in Pacifica, the Court in Sable explained that "the dial-it medium requires the listener to take affirmative steps to receive the communication. . . . Placing a telephone call is not the same as turning on a radio and being taken by surprise by an indecent message."[15] Because Internet communications were more similar to telephonic speech, whereby a user took affirmative steps to retrieve speech, a ban on indecent material was similarly inappropriate.

The Supreme Court also looked to previous land use zoning ordinance decisions which restricted the placement of adult movie theaters in residential neighborhoods. For example, in Renton v. Playtime Theaters, Inc.,[16] the Court declared that local governments may constitutionally restrict the placement of adult entertainment businesses. Such ordinances are legitimate when they are enacted to minimize the secondary effects of such establishments, such as increased crime and deteriorating property values which such businesses foster.

The Federal government asserted that the CDA was constitutional because it offered a type of "cyberzoning" to the Internet. The Court, however, found that because there were no analogous problems relating to the secondary effects of such speech involved on the Internet, the government could not legitimately restrict Internet speech. Moreover, the Court observed that the true rationale behind the enactment of the CDA was to limit the primary effects that indecent speech would have on children.

The Supreme Court also paid some attention to the vagueness of the CDA's wording. The Court was highly critical of the Congress' failure to include definitions either of the word, "indecent," or the phrase, "in context, depicts or describes, in terms patently offensive as measured by contemporary community standards, sexual or excretory activities or organs." It was additionally unclear to the Court how these two standards related to one another.

The Supreme Court has historically critically examined both content-based restrictions on speech and vaguely written criminal statutes. In Miller v. California,[17] the Supreme Court set forth its definition of what, precisely, may be considered obscene material. There the Court said that material would be considered obscene if it met all standards of a three-part test: "(a) whether the average person, applying contemporary community standards would find that the work, taken as a whole, appeals to the prurient interest; (b) whether the work depicts or describes, in a patently offensive way, sexual conduct specifically defined by the applicable state law; and (c) whether the work, taken as a whole, lacks serious literary, artistic, political, or scientific value."[18] The definitions included in the CDA are nowhere near as exact as those outlined in Miller. For example, the Court noted that the second part of the Miller test–that the material be specifically defined by state law–is absent in the CDA. Furthermore, the obscene material prohibited by Miller is only of a sexual nature. The CDA, on the other hand, extends its ban to "excretory activities" and to "organs" of an excretory nature.

Additionally, the CDA did not exempt from its ban works which had "serious literary, artistic, political or scientific value," material otherwise protected under Miller. Therefore, serious medical websites, such as on-line anatomy texts, or political web sites including those on AIDS activism, would have been outlawed by the CDA, even though they would not likely have been classified as obscene under the Supreme Court's traditional First Amendment framework. Moreover, the inclusion of the "community standards" criterion, the Court argued, meant that "any communication available to a nation-wide audience will be judged by the standards of the community most likely to be offended by the message."[19]

The Court has also historically found that restrictions on adult speech are unacceptable if less restrictive alternatives would achieve the same purpose that the statute was enacted to serve. Although the government may legitimately have an interest in protecting minors from harmful materials, that does not justify an unnecessarily broad ban on adult speech. The Court quoted from its opinion in Bolger v. Youngs Drug Products Corp.: "Regardless of the strength of the government's interest" in protecting children, "the level of discourse reaching a mailbox simply cannot be limited to that which would be suitable for a sandbox."[20] Here, the Court broadly asserted that current filtering software would go a long way toward protecting children without also limiting adult access.

The Court further rejected the Federal government's proffered defenses to the new criminal provisions. Although the Federal government asserted that one may have a defense to the crime of transmitting indecent material to a minor by using a credit card verification system, nothing would actually prevent children from using their parents' cards to register at a web site containing sexual material. The Court similarly rejected the defense that a web site owner would not be guilty if the site were "tagged" as a sexually explicit site. Such a tag would then be filtered by government-approved software. The Court rejected this as well, arguing that such tagging would be ineffective unless all Internet users employed such filtering software. The Court also noted that such "tagging" software had not yet been developed.

The Court declined to edit the CDA, as requested by the Federal government. Instead, the Court saved only the one part which passed constitutional muster: the section which prohibited the transmission of an "obscene" communication to minors. The rest of the statute was struck down.

Chief Justice Rehnquist and Justice O'Connor dissented in part. The two stressed that, at some future point, the Internet may be "zoned" just like a geographical community, thereby restricting indecent speech to its own corner of cyberspace. However, they allowed that because technological applications had not been fully developed, the CDA was currently unconstitutionally broad. The dissenters further found that the CDA could be partially salvaged if it proscribed the transmission of indecent material to minors if the author of the material knew that all of the recipients were children.

THE COURT'S TREATMENT OF THE INTERNET

One of the most striking features of ACLU v. Reno is the Court's analysis of the Internet. The justices traced the history and growth of the Internet from the original ARPANET of 1969 to the prediction that 200 million people will be using the Internet by 1999. They found that the web was "comparable, from the readers' viewpoint, to both a vast library including millions of readily available and indexed publications and a sprawling mall offering goods and services."[21] They further noted that the web constitutes a platform for speech which extends to a worldwide audience. Additionally, the Court stressed that anyone using the web can "publish" their home page to an international audience.

The Court's analysis of the Internet is significant because it provides judges and attorneys with some background knowledge of this rapidly expanding medium. Fortunately, this background picture was painted in very positive terms. Because the Court generally seemed to stress the global reach of the Internet, its user friendliness, and its similarity to traditional publishing, other courts will probably safeguard the positive tone of the Court's discussion and be fairly unwilling to allow government intervention of cyberspace.

COMMENTARY ON THE OPINION

Over the past year, commentators have taken issue with several facets of the Supreme Court's ruling. Although they generally argue that the result was correct, they observe that, for technical or legal reasons, the Court should have reached its decision on different grounds. They also note that Reno did not address several issues which have the potential to cause legal confusion at some future point.

Potential Problems Relating to Technology

The Supreme Court in Reno chose to extend its analysis of First Amendment jurisprudence by looking through the traditional lens of medium-specific analysis. That is, the Court looked to the functions and qualities of the medium of the expression in order to determine the invasiveness of the speech itself. For example, print media is afforded a high level of protection, while broadcasting is granted a comparatively lower level of protection. In Reno, the Court granted the Internet a very high level of protection, akin to print.

However, the same rationale for the Internet's protection may eventually cause some Internet applications to be comparatively unprotected. For example, would the Court have reached the same conclusion if web page designers were in the habit of linking to tawdry photographs, but without mentioning that the links were to indecent material? It is, after all, relatively simple to give a link a name other than the "official" name of the document to which it is linked. In this scenario, a child could easily stumble upon indecent material, even though that was clearly not the child's intention. The use of meta-tags in search engines may also allow children to unintentionally retrieve indecent material.

Similarly, the Court did not address "push" technologies which operate remarkably similarly to television. An Internet user can subscribe to web services which provide a stream of information sent by the site and displayed on the user's web browser. Microsoft's Internet Explorer 4.x browser goes so far as to call its "push" websites "channels." What happens when a web site "pushes" indecent material to its user's desktop, even though that user had originally believed that the site would provide only news, sports, or business content?

The Court also did not address the rapid increase of the availability of multimedia content on the Internet. Files are no longer necessarily in simple text, graphic, or hypertext formats. Instead, graphics may now be animated, and sound and video files can now be played on browser "plug-ins" provided free of charge. When accessing these special types of multimedia files, the Internet user has about as much control of content as a television viewer does.

Additionally, the recent advent of WebTV was neglected by the Court. The web could always be easily displayed on a large video screen in the family living room, although this has not happened in practice often–until recently with the creation and marketing of simple computers which are designed to run on a regular television. Thus, the Internet has the potential to be just as invasive to family life as is television broadcasting, a medium which enjoys much less First Amendment protection.

Some commentators assert that, in place of medium-specific analysis, the Court could have alternatively focused on whether the content of the speech has "the potential to contribute to the marketplace of ideas on any communications medium."[22] This would mean that the constitutionality of one's expression was not dependent on whether it was conveyed in print, by television, or by the Internet.

As the noted constitutional scholar Laurence H. Tribe wrote, it is "as if the Constitution had to be reinvented with the birth of each new technology."[23] Instead, commentators like Tribe argue that First

Amendment analysis should focus on whether the expression is constitutional by its very nature. Speech would be protected if a substantial government interest did not outweigh the interest in allowing a marketplace of ideas to flourish, and as long as the government interest was achieved using the least restrictive means necessary.

One advantage that such an analysis would have is that it prevents the inequity of results which a medium-specific analysis may have when applied to the Internet. For example, it is unlawful for broadcasters to transmit indecent material when children are watching over-air television, while the transmission of indecent material over the Internet during daylight hours is constitutionally protected, even when it is viewed on the family television. Confusion about the legality of the transmission of indecent, non-obscene material will likely grow as a result of the Court's continued use of medium-specific analysis in an age of technology where different media seem to be on a path of convergence and digital works become increasingly malleable.

Potential Legal Theory Problems

Another constitutional scholar, Eugene Volokh levels a more serious theoretical charge against the Supreme Court's reasoning, claiming that the Court failed to abide by its own standard.[24] The Supreme Court insisted that burdens on free speech are "unacceptable if less restrictive alternatives would be at least as effective in achieving the legitimate purpose that the statute was enacted to serve."[25] Volokh contends, and the Reno opinion does bear this out, that the Court summarily concluded that tagging and filtering software would be effective. The Court, however, never clearly analyzed how these technological measures would be "at least as effective" in protecting minors from indecent material. In fact, the Court stressed the opposite conclusion–that children could always access indecent web sites at homes not using this software, or by finding ways to turn off the software, thereby making this technology nowhere near as effective as a total ban. Volokh charges, then, that the Supreme Court created a new standard–that restrictive alternatives to speech would have to be "pretty much" (or "more or less") as effective as an outright ban.

The problem with what the Supreme Court ended up doing is that it creates a very poor yardstick for measuring what is "pretty much" effective. That is, courts will have wide latitude in measuring the effectiveness of alternative speech restrictions. Measurement will turn out to be a highly normative process, without any clear constitutional direction whatsoever.

Volokh contends that speech rights would be placed on a surer footing by creating a medium-neutral framework, like that discussed by Tribe, above. For example, the Court could create a "substantial burden is unconstitutional" approach: "If the law imposes a substantial burden on generally protected speech, then it is per se impermissible, even if this means we must sacrifice a significant amount of shielding of children."[26] However, modest burdens on speech may be permissible in order to shield children, or for other legitimate state ends. But, such a framework presupposes that the Court first outline what types of speech minors may legitimately have access to, an issue not well covered in Reno. Volokh also writes that this type of analysis necessitates a definition of what a substantial burden to speech would look like. Although these proposed guidelines would be subject to a great deal of scrutiny by the Court if ever adopted, it would minimize the current uncertainty stemming from the application of a medium-specific standard. It would further correct any misunderstandings about·the balancing test for burdened speech outlined, but not fully analyzed, in Reno.

The Court never reached a discussion of the proper jurisdictional framework for addressing disputes in cyberspace. In fact, the Court left untouched an assertion in the American Library Association brief stating that the CDA would be largely ineffective because Americans would still have access to indecent material posted from abroad.[27] It would be impractical to compel the extradition of foreign nationals who post such indecent material, especially if the material is lawful in the home country.

International issues in cyberspace will very likely multiply quickly. Even if content restrictions somehow become standardized, contractual, privacy, and intellectual property concerns are likely to be disputed, too. Legal scholars contend that nationally-based laws will not adequately resolve these issues because countries are seldom able to extend the power of their sovereignty outside their borders.[28] Instead, these international issues may be better addressed by separate global legal bodies, or, better still, technical standards agreed upon by the international community which address these problems.

Another legal area left unresolved by Reno is the protection of free speech rights in private, non-governmental fora. Government entities traditionally cannot restrict content, unless there is a significant state interest in doing so, as aptly demonstrated in Reno. However, the same standard does not always apply to private entities. For example, in the physical world, speech generally may be restricted indoors and in non-public areas, although speech in privately owned outdoor shopping centers and company-owned towns is afforded a great deal of protection.

There currently is no standard for protecting First Amendment rights in cyberspace areas not controlled by the government. That is, although the Federal government could not enact the CDA, there is no law preventing Internet service providers from carrying out the same ends, as long as they abide by their contract with users. One legal commentator argues that free speech rights should be extended to privately-owned realms of cyberspace, such as Internet service providers, because the Internet so closely parallels the permissible areas for free speech in the physical world.[29] Although Reno need not have decided this specific issue, it will likely be an uncertain legal area for some time.

Government Use of Filtering Software After Reno

Reno did not decide with any finality whether the use of filtering software by public libraries, or other government entities, is constitutional. One reading of Reno, however, is that if current software filters ban too much non-obscene material in an effort to exclude indecent material, then such software use is an unconstitutional government restriction on content. The Court in Reno found that "existing technology did not include any effective method for a sender to prevent minors from obtaining access on the Internet without also denying access to adults."[30] It is likely that the Court was thinking specifically of filtering software when making this assertion.

Nevertheless, software filters may be an acceptable solution if they are used only at terminals used by minors. The government has an interest in shielding children from offensive material, and may accomplish such a restriction without burdening adult speech rights. Adults, of course, would need to have access to terminals without filters.

Still others may argue that filtering software should be seen only as an extension of the library's collection development policy. Libraries, by their nature and mission, cannot collect all works by all authors, but instead try to acquire and retain those works which provide the greatest amount of accurate information to the greatest number of people at the least cost. Some would argue that only those Internet materials which are not filtered are suitable to add to the library's on-line collection. That is, only non-filtered materials are accurate and of high enough quality to add to the collection. This argument, though, rests on a slippery slope which may call into question a library's traditional selection process for print material. Moreover, a broad reading of Reno shows that the Court is exceedingly skeptical about prohibiting adult access to indecent material.

CONCLUSION

Reno v. ACLU will long be remembered as the Supreme Court case which extended First Amendment free speech rights to the Internet. The opinion itself is notable because of its discussion of Internet technology, as well as legal standards for the protection of speech rights. However, it spite of its landmark holding, legal scholars have taken issue with some of the underpinnings of the opinion, especially its use of medium-specific criteria to determine the permissibility of material. Judges, attorneys, and law professors will likely debate the merits and failings of Reno long into the next century. Nevertheless, the case currently stands as the first beacon to shed legal light on the newly networked world.

NOTES

1. 117 S. Ct. 2329 (1997).
2. 47 U.S.C.A. §223(a)(Supp. 1997).
3. Id.
4. 47 U.S.C.A §223(d).
5. 117 S. Ct. at.
6. Pub. L. 104, 100 Stat. 56.
7. Reno, 117 S. Ct. 2329 at note 24, quoting Cyberporn and Children: The Scope of the Problem, the State of the Technology, and the Need for Congressional Action, Hearing on S.892 before the Senate Committee on the Judiciary, 104th Cong., 1st Sess., 708 (1995).
8. 929 F.Supp. 824 (ED Pa. 1996).
9. 390 U.S. 629 (1968).
10. Id. at 646.
11. 438 U.S. 726 (1978).

12. Southeastern Promotions, Ltd. v. Conrad, 420 U.S. 546, 557 (1975).

13. 117 S.Ct. at.

14. 492 U.S. 115 (1989).

15. Sable, 492 U.S. at 127-28.

16. 475 U.S. 41 (1986).

17. 413 U.S. 15 (1973).

18. Id. at 24.

19. 117 S.Ct. at.

20. 463 U.S. 60, 74-75 (1983).

21. 117 S.Ct. at.

22. Stephen C. Jacques, Comment, Reno v. ACLU: Insulating the Internet, the First Amendment, and the Marketplace of Ideas, 46 Am. U.L. Rev. 1945, 1987 (1997).

23. Id. at 1987, quoting Laurence H. Tribe, The Constitution in Cyberspace: Law and Liberty Beyond the Electronic Frontier, Address at the First Conference on Computers, Freedom & Privacy (Mar. 26, 1991) <http://cpsr.org/cpsr/freespeech/tribeconstitutioncyberspace.txt>

24. Eugene Volokh, Freedom of Speech, Shielding Children, and Transcending Balancing, 1997 Sup. Ct. Rev. 141 (1998).

25. Reno, 117 S.Ct. at 2348.

26. Volokh at 172.

27. 117 S.Ct. 2329 at note 45. The Court found that the CDA was overly-broad as written; therefore, it declined to address this issue.

28. Joel R. Reidenberg, Lex Informatica: The Formulation of Information Policy Rules Through Technology, 76 Texas L. Rev. 553 (1998).

29. David J. Goldstone, A Funny Thing Happened On the Way to the Cyber Forum: Public vs. Private in Cyberspace Speech, 69 U. Colo. L. Rev. 1 (1998).

30. 117 S.Ct. at.

TAXES AND TORTS

Taxes and the Self-Employed Author

Sheila D. Foster

Poems on scraps of paper journals in composition books, stories on tissue paper, songs on the backs of napkins–many people today write for personal pleasure. Others work in professions or for companies where they are paid a salary or an hourly wage by an employer for their written work. However, more and more Americans–including writers–by choice or through corporate down-sizing, are becoming entrepreneurial in their outlook and taking the self-employment road.

Taxpayers who work for an employer are able to deduct on Schedule A of their personal tax return the unreimbursed expenses associated with their work that exceed 2% of their adjusted gross income. If the total of unreimbursed business-related expenses does not exceed 2% of adjusted gross income, no deduction is allowed.

What of writers who are not employed by others? Like those who

Sheila D. Foster is Associate Professor and Director of the MBA program at The Citadel in Charleston, SC. Dr. Foster holds a BS from Radford University, an MEd from Virginia Commonwealth University, and a PhD from Virginia Polytechnic Institute and State University.

[Haworth co-indexing entry note]: "Taxes and the Self-Employed Author." Foster, Sheila D. Co-published simultaneously in *The Acquisitions Librarian* (The Haworth Information Press, an imprint of The Haworth Press, Inc.) No. 26, 2001, pp. 145-153; and: *Publishing and the Law: Current Legal Issues* (ed: A. Bruce Strauch) The Haworth Information Press, an imprint of The Haworth Press, Inc., 2001, pp. 145-153. Single or multiple copies of this article are available for a fee from The Haworth Document Delivery Service [1-800-342-9678, 9:00 a.m. - 5:00 p.m. (EST). E-mail address: getinfo@haworthpressinc.com].

pursue other hobbies, "pleasure writers" find little help in the tax code for their activities. However, once a person begins to earn income from writing, the U.S. tax code offers ways to shelter income and use expenses incurred to reduce taxable income.

Even if gross income is not as much as the filing requirement for his/her filing status and age and he/she would otherwise not be required to file an income tax return, the self-employed writer who earns net income (gross income less expenses) of $400 or more from his/her works must report that income to the Internal Revenue Service. Although some self-employed writer/taxpayers choose to operate as either a regular C-corporation or as an S-corporation, many choose not to incorporate and instead to report the income earned from their works on Schedule C or Schedule C-EZ as part of their personal income tax return, Form 1040, that is filed each April 15th.

If the writer has more than one source of self-employment income during the year, the net self-employed incomes are combined, and if the total is more than $400, that income is subject to self-employment tax. This tax, reported on Schedule E of the personal income tax return, is composed of two parts: Old Age, Survivor, and Disability Insurance (OASDI) and Medicare Hospital Insurance. Together these are comparable to Social Security tax withheld on an employee and matched by the employer.

If both husband and wife are self-employed, their incomes are not aggregated for purposes of calculating self-employment tax. Instead, the self-employed income from all sources is calculated for each separately in determining if the $400 threshold has been met [Section 6017]. Until recently, if the taxpayer found that self-employment income was going to be slightly more than $400, he/she might consider hiring his/her spouse as an employee in the business because the spouse's income was subject to neither Social Security nor self-employment taxes. However, this practice is no longer permitted and the spouse's income is subject to Social Security taxes. Therefore, writer/taxpayers who have used this method of reducing self-employment tax may want to reconsider the benefits of continuing this practice.

Expenses generally may be used to reduce gross income if they are incurred in a profit-motivated activity–i.e., if the author is trying to make a profit or earn a living from his/her work. Once the activity of writing becomes profit-motivated, deductions are allowed which will reduce the gross income to a net amount. The Internal Revenue Service may use a number of factors to determine whether the activity is profit-motivated, but an activity that has net income, gross income in excess of expenses, for any two of five consecutive years is presumed to be profit-motivated [Reg. Sec. 1.183(c)(ii)]. Other factors that may be considered (if the writing does not produce net income during two out of five consecutive years) include:

- whether the writer acted in a business-like manner,
- the expertise of the writer,
- the time and effort the writer devoted to the activity,
- the taxpayer's history of income or loss associated with writing,
- the success of the writer in carrying on similar or dissimilar activities,
- the amount of occasional profits,
- the financial status of the taxpayer,
- and any element of personal pleasure and recreation that might be derived from the activity [Reg. Sec. 1.183-2(b)].

To be deductible, expenses must be:

- business related (not of a personal nature),
- an expense of the taxpayer (not of someone else),
- ordinary,
- necessary (though not necessarily indispensable),
- reasonable in amount,
- and properly documented [Sec. 162 and Sec. 212].

Clearly, if the writing is deemed to be profit-motivated, amounts paid for such expenses as paper supplies used for writing, secretarial help for typing up the author's writings, postage to mail articles to a publisher, photography costs for jacket covers, and automobile and travel expense to promote the work would be deductible. Other deductions and the restrictions or limitations on them may not be quite so clear.

Most self-employed taxpayers are aware that they may be able to take a home office deduction. This deduction is allowed only if the office is used exclusively on a regular basis as the taxpayer's principle place of business [Sec. 280A(c)(l)]. The terms "exclusively" and "on a regular basis" are important. The guest room where Aunt Martha stays when she comes to visit every few months probably would not qualify as being used exclusively even though the room is used as an office the rest of the time. Likewise, a room used exclusively as an office by a writer who practices the craft only a few days each year or who brings work home from the workplace each day probably would not qualify as being used on a regular basis. The Taxpayer Relief Act of 1997 made this deduction available to many taxpayers who had previously been unable to use it by expanding the definition of "principal place of business" to mean that "(1) the office is used by the taxpayer to conduct administrative and management activities of the taxpayer's trade or business; and (2) there is no other fixed location where the taxpayer conducts" such activities. If the writer/taxpayer is entitled to the deduction, then a portion of the rent or depreciation of cost (of the house–not the land), utilities, insurance, repairs, real estate taxes, etc., may be deducted as a business expense against writing income. The portion that may be deducted is frequently based on the square footage used for the office compared to the total square footage of the home. The deduction for a home office, however, may not exceed the *gross profit* from the business. *Gross profit* in this case is the net income (income less expenses) from the business plus any gain attributable to the office if the house is sold during the tax year. In simple terms, in most years the writer/taxpayer calculates net income from the business without taking into consideration any deduction for a home office. The deduction for the home office then can be used to reduce that figure, but can only reduce it to zero. The home office cannot cause the business to have a loss for the year. Any home office deduction that cannot be used in the current year because of this limitation may be carried forward indefinitely to future years to reduce future self-employment income.

Not all expenses related to the writer's work, however, are deductible for income tax purposes. Capital expenditures are not deductible expenses. A capital asset is property that is used in the business, has a useful life of more than one year, and wears out, becomes obsolete, or loses value over time or with use. Additionally, any amount paid that prolongs the life of, increases the value of, or adapts property for new or different uses is considered a capital expenditure. Capital assets and capital expenditures generally must be depreciated or amortized, using Form 4562, over the useful life of the asset rather than being deducted in total in one year [Reg. Sec. 1.263(a)-1(b)]. In some cases, a Section 179 deduction, also reported on Form 4562, allows the taxpayer to deduct the entire cost of the asset (up to $18,000 for certain qualifying property) in the first year rather than to deduct a part of the cost over several years. A Section 179 deduction cannot exceed the income derived from the activity in which the asset is used and, therefore, much like the deduction for a home office, cannot be used to create a loss from that activity. Any portion of the deduction that cannot be used because of the income limitation may be carried over to the following year making the amount that could be deducted the second year $18,000 plus the amount unused the year before. Because of the complexity of the tax laws regarding depreciation deductions, the writer may need to seek professional advice.

From time to time, writers may face somewhat unique situations that can affect their income tax liability. For example, occasionally authors will choose to live abroad while they write or as they prepare to write. If the period of residency in a foreign country is long, the writer may need or want to work in that country. There may be tax incentives for such taxpayers. U.S. citizens are generally taxed on all income from whatever source derived, including income derived from sources outside the United States. Income earned abroad might also be subject to taxation by the host country where it was earned. This could result in double taxation of the individual. In order to alleviate this problem, the tax code has provided two alternatives–the foreign tax credit and the foreign-earned income tax exclusion.

In lieu of a foreign-earned income tax exclusion, the writer/taxpayer who earns income abroad may claim a foreign tax credit [Sec. 164(a)(3)]. The credit equals the lesser of foreign taxes paid (or accrued) and the portion of U.S. tax liability attributable to the income earned in all foreign countries. The taxpayer first calculates both foreign tax paid on foreign income and U.S. tax liability (before credits) on worldwide income. The taxpayer prorates the U.S. liability between U.S. income and foreign-earned income. Based on this prorating, the portion of U.S. liability attributable to foreign income is compared to the amount of foreign taxes paid or accrued, and the taxpayer claims the lesser amount as a credit on his/her U.S. income tax return. For example, assume that a taxpayer had a total of $50,000 in earned income for one tax year. Assume also that the same taxpayer earned $30,000 in the U.S., $20,000 in a foreign country, paid $2,000 in income taxes to that foreign country, and had a U.S. tax liability of $14,000 before credits on the $50,000 of worldwide income. Forty percent, or $20,000, of the worldwide income of $50,000 was earned in a foreign country. Therefore, 40%, or $5,600 of the $14,000 U.S. liability is attributable to the foreign income. The taxpayer could therefore claim a foreign-tax credit of $2,000, or the lesser of the $2,000 paid to the foreign country and the $5,600 U.S. tax liability attributable to the foreign income. In this case, because the amount paid to the foreign country is much less than the pro rata portion of the U.S. tax associated with the foreign income, the taxpayer may want to consider the foreign-earned income tax exclusion.

Under the foreign-earned income tax exclusion, the taxpayer files a U.S. tax return and excludes part or all of the income earned abroad instead of claiming a credit for taxes that were paid to a foreign government. Under the provisions of Section 911, the first $72,000 earned in 1998 ($74,000 in 1999, $76,000 in 2000; $78,000 in 2001; and $80,000 in 2002 and thereafter [Tax Payer Relief Act of 1997]) in a foreign country may be excluded for gross income in lieu of taking the foreign tax credit. For a married couple, if both have foreign-earned income, each may claim the exclusion. The exclusion does not apply to pensions, annuities, salary paid by the U.S. government, or to deferred compensation. This means that the writer/taxpayer cannot choose to live abroad after retirement, receive a pension, and exclude that pension from U.S. gross income for tax purposes [Sec. 911(b)(1) (B)]. To be eligible, the writer must either be a bona fide resident of, or be physically present 330 days during the year in one or more foreign countries. Because living expenses are frequently greater in foreign countries, a deduction for housing costs that exceed 16% of gross salary is allowed as part of the foreign-earned income tax exclusion.

Deductible expenses also may not be related to tax-exempt income, may not be specifically disallowed by tax law, and may not be for things that are illegal or in violation of public policy. While it would be unlikely that the first two prohibitions would affect the working writer in connection with his/her work, the last one might arise under certain circumstances. For example, in the writing of an article on a foreign country's economic conditions, the author might be asked for a "bribe" by a foreign official in order to secure that information because that "is how things are done" in that country. However, bribes and kickbacks to federal, state, local, or foreign officials or employees are specifically prohibited [Sec. 162 (c)(1)]. Likewise, if a writer parks in the wrong place or for too long a period of time in order to be in the right place at the right time for a breaking story and receives a parking ticket, the fine or penalty is not deductible [Sec. 162(f)].

Although some items that the writer taxpayer might think would be deductible are not, other expenses that seem less likely to be deductible are allowed under current tax law. Three allowable deductions that are sometimes missed by self-employed taxpayers are the deductions for health insurance payments, for self-employment tax payments, and for Keogh, self-employed SEP, and SIMPLE plans. These three are deductions for *adjusted gross income* and are reported on the front of Form 1040 rather than on Schedule C or C-EZ. (The difference is that these three reduce adjusted gross income, affect limits on Schedule A, and reduce taxable income but do not reduce self-employment income and the self-employment tax liability.)

Health insurance premiums are ordinarily included among itemized deductions on Schedule A and are deductible only to the extent that medical expenses exceed 7.5% of adjusted gross income. In most cases, the self-employed taxpayer may deduct 40% (up from 30% in previous years) of the health insurance premiums they pay for themselves and their immediate family as a deduction *for adjusted gross income* [Sec. 106]. As a result, the taxpayer can deduct 40% of the premiums even if medical expenses on Schedule A were not high enough otherwise to have allowed any deduction. Premiums for long-term health care are also deductible if the writer/taxpayer is not eligible for long-term health care provided by an employer.

The self-employed writer pays self-employment tax in lieu of the Social Security that would be withheld if he/she received a salary. The amount paid is equal to the combined employee and employer Social Security payment (7.65% paid by the employee; 7.65% paid by the employer; total of 15.3% paid) that would be made if the writer worked for a company. Self-employment tax is 12.4% on the first $65,400 ($68,400 in 1998) for OASDI and 2.9% on all self-employment income for Medicare H for a total of 15.3%. As with health insurance, for the self-employed writer/taxpayer a portion, 50%, of this tax is deductible for *adjusted gross income* [Sec. 164(f)]. The result of this is that the self-employed taxpayer may deduct 50% of the 15.3% paid while the taxpayer who works for a wage or salary receives no such deduction.

Keogh, SEP and SIMPLE retirement plans offer significant advantages and are available for the self-employed taxpayer and his/her employees. The taxpayer/writer can contribute to his/her own account as well as that of employees and thereby reduce the profitability of the business and both the self-employment and personal income tax liabilities. The accounts grow on a tax-deferred basis and do not generate taxable income to the taxpayer/writer or to the employees until distributions are received from the plan. However, to be a qualified retirement plan, the plans must be made available to eligible employees as well as the taxpayer. Because of cost associated with making retirement plan contributions for all eligible employees due to the participatory nature of these plans, many writer/taxpayers may find that contributions to an IRA (Individual Retirement Account) are a better choice. If the taxpayer chooses to use the Keogh, SEP or SIMPLE plan, filing and reporting deadlines must be strictly observed for the plan to remain eligible as a deduction *for adjusted gross income.*

One problem that is unique to self-employed (when compared to salaried) writers is tax treatment of the income associated with selling their works. Authors may choose to obtain a private copyright on their works. It might seem logical to the author to assume that such a valuable asset would be considered a capital asset for tax purposes, resulting in more favorable tax treatment in terms of depreciation and capital gains consideration at the time of sale. However, the U.S. Tax code states that " . . . [T]he term 'capital asset' means property held by the taxpayer (whether or not connected with his trade or business), but does not include . . . a copyright, a literary, musical, or artistic composition, . . . or similar property, held by . . . a taxpayer whose personal efforts created such property" [Section 1221(3)(a)]. "Similar property" is a broadly defined term including such things as "a theatrical production, a radio program, a newspaper cartoon strip, or any other property eligible for copyright protection . . . but does not include a patent or an invention, or a design which may be protected only under the patent law and not under the copyright law" [Reg. Section 1.1221-1(c)(1)].

This section of the Code requires that the author who sells his/her own work must report the proceeds from that sale as ordinary income rather than as a capital gain. With a maximum income tax rate of 39.6% and a capital gains tax rate of 28%, the difference in income tax liability can be quite large. For example, if an asset is sold for $100,000, the federal income tax would be $3,960 if the proceeds were treated as ordinary income but would be only $2,800 if the proceeds were treated as capital gains. Unfortunately, the writer/taxpayer has no choice in this case and must report the sale as ordinary income even though it results in a greater income tax liability.

The income of writers who are self-employed is affected by more income tax laws than that of the writer who is employed by another and who receives income from his/her writing in the form of a salary or wage. Deductions for expenses, both from and for adjusted gross income, exist that can be used to lower the reportable net income for both self-employment and income tax purposes. Some expenses that the self-employed writer encounters that would appear to be deductible either are not allowed or are limited by a dollar amount or some other form of cap. Income tax law is complicated and income taxes may not seem important to the self-employed writer–until April 15th draws near each year. At that time it is frequently too late to do any tax planning that will enable the taxpayer to report lower taxable income. However, with good tax planning throughout the year, the writer/taxpayer may be able to substantially (and legitimately) reduce tax liability. Unless the taxpayer is up to date on the tax laws, it might be wise to seek the help of a professional who can help the taxpayer take advantage of all allowable deductions and credits in order to pay the lowest legal tax.

The Tort Liability of Publishers

A. Bruce Strauch

"It is a prized American privilege to speak one's mind, although not always with perfect good taste, on all public institutions."[1] The very First Amendment added part and parcel with the adoption of the U.S. Constitution guarantees this privilege as a primary defense of democracy. "To many this is, and always will be, folly; but we have staked upon it our all."[2]

The First Amendment, however, has never been an absolute guarantee of publishing whatever one pleased. The Bill of Rights was intended to restrict the power of government. It was government which was to pass no laws abridging freedom of speech and the press. Publishers were to be so free of *government* interference that they were even allowed to advocate violence, certainly the only tenable position following the American Revolution.

That there is some limit to free speech, however, is easily understood. The ordinary citizen is not at the mercy of out-of-control publishers for purposes of ridicule or community shame with utter impunity. Such offenses as defamation, invasion of privacy, obscenity, incitement and fighting words were always outside the protective shield of the First Amendment. "[O]pportunists, for private gain, cannot be permitted to arm themselves with . . . a free press, and proceed to use it as an iron standard to smooth their path by crushing the living

---

A. Bruce Strauch is Associate Professor of Business Law at The Citadel, Charleston, SC. He practised tort law for fifteen years, has published numerous books and articles including works of fiction, and is the publisher of *Against the Grain*, the trade journal of the scholarly publishing industry.

[Haworth co-indexing entry note]: "The Tort Liability of Publishers." Strauch, A. Bruce. Co-published simultaneously in *The Acquisitions Librarian* (The Haworth Information Press, an imprint of The Haworth Press, Inc.) No. 26, 2001, pp. 155-172; and: *Publishing and the Law: Current Legal Issues* (ed: A. Bruce Strauch) The Haworth Information Press, an imprint of The Haworth Press, Inc., 2001, pp. 155-172. Single or multiple copies of this article are available for a fee from The Haworth Document Delivery Service [1-800-342-9678, 9:00 a.m. - 5:00 p.m. (EST). E-mail address: getinfo@haworthpressinc.com].

rights of others to privacy and repose."[3] Relieving the press of responsibility would be "ultimately harmful to the permanent good health of the press itself."[4]

The Constitution was adopted along with the entire body of the Common Law of England among which was tort law–the law of wrongful injury. The publisher is protected by the Constitution from government; the ordinary citizen is protected from the publisher by the law of tort.[5]

While the publisher committing English common law torts is fair game for the tort lawyers, of necessity, a balance must be struck lest the tort lawyers achieve an effect that government may not–to stifle the publisher through fear of suit.

Thus, in an effort to protect robust free speech and publishing, the courts have largely shielded publishers from general tort liability. The theory is that "[w]hat a State may not constitutionally bring about by means of a criminal statute is likewise beyond the reach of its civil law[.]"[6] A fear of tort liability may just as effectively curtail speech and the free flow of ideas through self-censorship as a criminal statute might.[7]

The 11th century Norman conquest of England brought a Viking French vocabulary into the English language. As the new ruling class, the Normans conducted the operations of the law in what was called Law French. "Tort" in French–wrong, fault, harm, injury, injustice–in the civil law means a wrongful injury. The victim can sue for a remedy of money damages. Torts fall into three categories: intentional, negligence and strict tort liability.

INTENTIONAL TORTS

Intentional torts are exactly as they sound–the injury is done deliberately.

Defamation

The tort of defamation is a false communication that injures a person's reputation through disgrace and diminished respect. When spoken, a defamation is called slander. Libel is a written false statement but has been extended to communications by electronic media with equal or even greater power than the printed word.

New York Times Co. v. Sullivan,[8] is probably the most widely cited case on the subject of libel of public figures. In March, 1960, the *Times* carried a full page advertisement entitled "Heed Their Rising Voices" which protested the treatment of civil rights protestors in Alabama. One paragraph stated that students who sang "My Country, 'Tis of Thee" on the State Capitol Steps were expelled from Alabama State College and the campus ringed by police.

L. B. Sullivan was one of three Commissioners of the City of Montgomery, Alabama and among his duties was supervision of the police department. He sued the *Times* claiming he was libeled by charges that he had answered peaceful protest with violence and intimidation. Some of the statements were indeed inaccurate. The police did not ring the campus in connection with the singing on the Capitol steps and the students were expelled, not for that incident, but for demanding service at a lunch counter. The *Times* admitted it ran the ad without making an effort to confirm the accuracy of the advertisement by checking the facts against news stories it had published.[9]

The Supreme Court stated the rationale for the First Amendment as assuring ". . . unfettered interchange of ideas for the bringing about of political and social changes desired by the people."[10] It "presupposes that right conclusions are more likely to be gathered out of a multitude of tongues, than through any kind of authoritative selection."[11]

The Court identified the advertisement as an expression of protest on a major political issue of the time and as such exactly the kind of free discussion that merited Constitutional protection. The question that had to be answered was whether certain false statements in the ad took it outside that protection.[12]

If defamation is the communication of a false statement, a true statement can never be defamation. The Court, however, was deeply bothered by self-censorship in the area of public debate. Critics of official action would be deterred by the fear that they could not prove that what they had said was true. Thus, it ruled that public officials could only recover damages for libel in the event of actual malice. It must be proved that the false statement was made with knowledge of its falsity or with reckless disregard of whether it was false.[13]

The Court further found that the failure of the *Times* to check all the facts in the ad against their own news stories was negligent rather than reckless. The *Times* had relied upon its knowledge of those sponsoring the ad as persons of good reputation. This is not particularly helpful as a guide to publishers on the question of what is reckless conduct because the Court dwelled at greater length on the extremely tenuous connection between Sullivan–who was not actually named in the ad–and the fairly minor inaccuracies in the ad.[14]

Note that *New York Times* stands for a requirement of malice in the defamation of *public figures*. The colloquial meaning of malice as "spite" or "ill-will" is not an element of that standard.[15] Liability is not imposed based on hatred but because of false statements of fact knowingly made.

Also note that in the case of *private figures*, simple negligence in printing false statements can be enough to establish liability.[16] The theory is that "falsehood is more easily tolerated where public attention creates the strong likelihood of a competition among ideas."[17] Public figures assume the risk by entering the public arena and have a ready audience waiting to hear their rebuttal. Non-public figures face much greater difficulty in finding a forum to refute falsehoods and the public has so little interest in them that they cannot hold attention long enough for the truth to prevail. Further, they are reluctant to initiate a rebuttal due to fear of increasing the harmful exposure.[18]

This is a tricky area because the Supreme Court has created a further category of ordinary people catapulted into the public view by becoming part of newsworthy events. Thus we have *private figures* of *public interest*. This is to the advantage of the publisher because the *New York Times* standard of recklessness rather than negligence in checking facts applies. The Court declined to

> saddle the press with the impossible burden of verifying to a certainty the facts associated in news articles with a person's name, picture or portrait, particularly as related to nondefamatory matter especially when the content of the speech itself afford no warning of prospective harm to another through falsity. A negligence test would place on the press the intolerable burden of guessing how a jury might assess the reasonableness of steps taken by it to verify the accuracy of every reference to a name, picture or portrait.[19]

Invasion of Privacy

Publishers avoid defamation by publishing the truth. They nonetheless may fall into liability based upon *invasion of privacy*.

The right to privacy was guaranteed by English common law and is found in the Constitution. The Fourth Amendment search and seizure provisions make the citizen safe at home and on the street from government intrusion.[20] Privacy rights are also found in the "penumbras" or shadows of the First, Third, Fourth, Fifth and Ninth Amendments.[21] Interestingly, Warren and Brandeis in a Harvard Law Review article of 1890 argued that it was the excesses of the press that made vital a right to privacy distinct from defamation.[22]

There are four distinct types of invasion of privacy: (1) intrusion upon seclusion, (2) public disclosure of private facts about someone's personal life, (3) appropriation of one's name or likeness for commercial purposes, and (4) publicity that places someone in a "false light" in the public eye.[23]

Protecting the sanctity and tranquility of the home is a high value.[24] Likewise we expect some basic right to go about our business and walk the streets without being stalked by the press.[25]

An *intrusion into seclusion* requires the following elements:

1. an intentional intrusion
2. upon the solitude or private affairs of another
3. if the intrusion would be highly offensive to the ordinary reasonable person.

In *Wolfson v. Lewis*,[26] two broadcast journalists were refused an interview with a health insurer CEO about his high salary. In an attempt to make him come to terms, they placed his home under surveillance using telescopes, zoom lens video cameras and ultra sensitive microphones and followed him to Florida where he had gone to evade them. They also intended an "ambush" in which they would approach the CEO or members of his family and shout embarrassing questions to get their reaction on film.

The "First Amendment does not guarantee the press a constitutional right of special access to information not available to the public generally."[27] News must be gathered by means within the law and without special privileges to invade the privacy of others.

The Court granted an injunction against the broadcasters, finding that they "undertook a course of hounding, harassing, intimidating, and frightening conduct in complete and blatant disregard" of tranquility and solitude in the home.[28] This tort typically would not apply to events in a public place.

> Thus there is no liability for the examination of a public record concerning the plaintiff, or of documents that the plaintiff is required to keep and make available for public inspection. Nor is there liability for observing him or even taking his photograph, while he is walking on the public highway, since he is not then in seclusion, and his appearance is public and open to the public eye. Even in a public place, however, there may be matters about the plaintiff, such as his underwear or the lack of it, that are not exhibited to the public gaze; and there may still be invasion of privacy when there is intrusion upon these matters.[29]

Nonetheless, stalking someone in public in a persistent course of hounding and harassment which becomes a substantial burden on the victim can be an intrusion.[30]

A typical *appropriation* case involves the unauthorized use of a celebrity's name in advertising. It's not hard to see the justice of this one in the world of celebrity endorsement of products and celebrity name franchises. Gold medals are barely hung around Olympic athletes' necks before the speculation begins on how much they will make from endorsing products. The unauthorized use of a celebrity's name for purposes of trade would unjustly enrich the pirate and reduce the celebrity's ability to earn a living as an entertainer.

In *Motschenbacher v. R.J. Reynolds Tobacco Company*,[31] a question of fact arose over whether a "likeness" of a race car driver was used in a Winston cigarette ad. No driver was recognizable in the picture, a spoiler had been added to the racing car and the number changed from "11" to "71." Nonetheless, distinctive decorations on the car caused avid race fans to identify the car as Motschenbacher's and he derived part of his living from endorsing commercial products.

In *Zacchini v. Scripps-Howard Broadcasting Co.*,[32] a human cannonball act at a county fair in Ohio was filmed by a TV station and shown in its entirety on the evening news. Zacchini, the cannonball, performed for hire. The broadcast of the entire act diminished the economic value of his performance by allowing people to watch TV for free rather than paying to attend the fair.

The U.S. Supreme Court noted that entertainment is often news, and news enjoys First Amendment protection. Nonetheless, Zacchini was entitled to reap the rewards of his commercial stake in his act.[33] Moreover, the protection of Zacchini's act encourages him to invest his time and effort to provide entertainment for the public. The same theory lies behind patent and copyright. Personal gain is the best encouragement of individual effort, and this in turn advances the public welfare.[34]

Some states hold that an invasion of privacy through placing someone in a *false light* requires the same elements as a defamation.[35] Others find it exists when a true (i.e., nondefamatory) statement is made but the intent is to create an insulting image.[36] For example, a photo of Elizabeth Taylor drinking in a nightclub is a fact, but the publisher's intent is for readers to picture her as a pathetic lush.

Outrage

Outrage is shorthand for the tort of the *Intentional Infliction of Emotional Distress*. The elements are easily understood. Someone

1. intentionally sets about
2. causing emotional distress to another
3. that action is severe and outrageous and should not be tolerated in a civilized society
4. the distress inflicted is beyond what a reasonable person should be expected to bear.

This tort is not intended to take the place of the other common law torts but can result from a composite of them.

If one can show (1) an uncivilized objective or (2) a civilized objective but an uncivilized method of achieving the result when a painless way would achieve the same result, then the case is easily made.

In the field of publishing, this tort has turned up in the area of paparazzi (literally, annoying insects–gadflies) stalking celebrities and most notably in the case of Jackie Onassis and her photog tormentor Ron Galella.[37] For a period of years, Galella brazenly forced Mrs. Onassis and her children to endure a continuous stream of tortious assaults, batteries, invasions of privacy and commercial exploitations of their personalities. Wherever they were, there he would be. He drove recklessly close to them in cars when they were on bicycles and horses. He chased them in motorboats and bribed people to tip him as to their whereabouts. This went on from the time the children were in grade school up through their college graduations. Galella and his teams followed them relentlessly, all the while carrying on in the distinctive paparazzo manner designed to irritate, frighten and infuriate the victims and thus produce unusual pictures. This was described as jumping, lunging, dashing at them, touching, bumping, scuffling, blocking and circling, all the while keeping up a constant stream of inane, goading or insulting patter. He followed them so closely that he was found to have "insinuated himself into the very fabric of Mrs. Onassis' life."[38]

Aiding and Abetting

The same act may be both a crime and a civil tort, and in the case of an intentional tort often is–for example, if I without provocation hit you on the head with a big stick. The criminal law punishes and deters; the civil law provides a remedy for the injured victim. Since most hoodlums have no money, the victim typically must be content with the punishment of the criminal law. But publishers are available as a deep pocket in some cases.

In *Rice v. Paladin Enterprises*[39] a wrongful death action was brought against The Paladin Press, publisher of *Hit Man*, a how-to-do book on hiring, or performing as, a professional killer. The book was extremely cold-blooded and provided detailed instructions which a killer followed to brutally murder a mother, her eight-year-old quadriplegic son and the son's nurse. He did this as a "hit man" for an ex-husband who wanted the $2 million settlement from the accident which had crippled his son.[40]

Maryland law naturally made aiding and abetting a killer a crime, but also provided for a civil action as well. A defendant may be civilly liable if he "by any means (words, signs, or motions) encourage[s], incite[s], aid[s], or abet[s] the act of the direct perpetrator of the tort."[41] A conspiracy or prearranged concert of action is not required; only that the defendant should advocate or encourage the commission of the crime.[42]

Prior to trial, Palladin Press took the extraordinary step of stipulating that it not only knew its book might be used by killers, but that it intended this result and in fact assisted the killer in this case. The sole issue before the court was whether the First Amendment posed an absolute bar on liability of a publisher in assisting criminal acts.[43]

The Supreme Court has held that the First Amendment protects the abstract advocacy of lawlessness.[44] However, the constitutional freedom of speech does not extend to speech or writing which becomes an integral part of a criminal act. This speech-act doctrine has been applied in every federal circuit.[45]

The Fourth Circuit found *Hit Man* to be exactly the kind of speech left unprotected by the Supreme Court and described by Justice Douglas in *Dennis v. United States.* "If this were a case where those who claimed protection under the First Amendment were teaching the techniques of sabotage . . . I would have no doubts. The freedom to speak is not absolute; the teaching of methods of terror . . . should be beyond the pale . . . "[46]

Ultimately, Paladin is a very narrow issue probably only applicable to those who publish how-to-do books on making fertilizer bombs. "*Hit Man* is not political manifesto, not revolutionary diatribe, not propaganda, advocacy, or protest, not an outpouring of conscience of credo."

"It contains no discussions of ideas, no argument, no information about politics, religion, science, art, or culture . . . it offers no agenda for self-governance, no insight into the issues of the day."[47]

"*Hit Man* is, pure and simple, a step-by-step murder manual, a training book for assassins."[48,49]

Paladin argued that a finding of liability in this case would expose news publishers equally in the case of mimickry and copycat conduct. The court observes to the contrary that the requisite intent to aid and abet will never be present. "In only the rarest case, as here where the publisher has stipulated in almost taunting defiance that it intended to assist murderers and other criminals . . . " would such evidence exist for a jury.[50]

NEGLIGENCE TORTS

Negligence is conduct that creates an unreasonable risk of harm to others. It is not done intentionally, but rather because you did not stop and think before you acted. Negligence requires a showing of three elements: Duty, the Act of Negligence, and that negligent act was the Proximate Cause of injury.

In *McCollum v. CBS, Inc.,*[51] an emotionally unstable teenage alcoholic committed suicide after listening to Ozzy Osbourne music. One of the songs, "Suicide Solution," contained the message that suicide was the only solution for an alcoholic. "Where to hide, Suicide is the only way out."[52]

The *duty* to not be negligent arises out of action. Whenever you act, you are obliged to look down the road and think about the consequences. CBS acted by publishing "Suicide Solution."

To be *negligent* is to fail to take reasonable care under the circumstances. This level of care is a balancing test between the cost of the care and the potential risk of injury if it is not taken.

To incite is to use words to stir up, spur on, urge someone to action.[53] To incite a teenager to hurt himself or others is arguably a negligent act. There are only two possible outcomes–he will or he won't hurt himself–and one of them is bad.

Applying the balancing test, it costs zero dollars to refrain from inciting someone–just keep your mouth shut–and the risk of suicide is that it's dreadfully fatal.

Mere advocacy of violence, however, is protected speech under the First Amendment.[54] To be outside that protection, (1) the music must have been intended to bring about suicide–Ozzy was trying to incite suicide–and (2) the music was likely to produce such a result.

Judges determine the law; juries determine the facts of the case. Where there is a question of fact, the case should go to the jury. Whether the music was an incitement would seem to be a jury question. Nonetheless, the *McCollum* court held that music lyrics did not contain the "call to action" required of an incitement.[55]

"Reasonable persons understand musical lyrics and poetic conventions as the figurative expressions which they are. No rational person would or could believe otherwise nor would they mistake musical lyrics and poetry for literal commands or directives to immediate action. To do so would indulge a fiction which neither common sense nor the First Amendment will permit."[56]

To be liable, a publisher's actions must be the direct or *proximate cause* of the injury. But for the publication, the injury would never have happened. There can in fact be two or more proximate causes if each was a *substantial factor* in causing the injury. A basic test is to drop out one of the actors and see if the injury would still occur.

But for the music, the boy would be alive today. But for his emotionally fragile state–but for his drinking–he would be alive today. Was the music in fact a necessary element in creating the suicide?

The second element of proximate cause is the question of *foreseeability*. There is no liability if a publisher could not reasonably foresee the consequences of his actions. If you cannot foresee, then how could you possibly prevent?

Does evidence of the rising level of teenage suicide provide foreseeability? The court held to the contrary. "Reasonable persons understand musical lyrics and poetic conversations as the figurative expressions which they are. No rational person would or could believe otherwise nor would they mistake musical lyrics and poetry for literal commands or directives to immediate action."[57]

The *McCollum* court essentially was saying a publisher has no ability to foresee all the potential reactions of unreasonable listeners and readers. Balancing the need for art against the impossibility of foreseeing the results of art, it could hold as a matter of law there was no way a jury should find art the proximate cause of injury.[58]

By contrast, in *Weirum v. RKO General, Inc.*,[59] a live radio broadcast urged listeners to intercept a disc jockey who was broadcasting live and moving among various locations. A prize was offered. In hurrying to locate him, two teenagers crashed into another and killed him. The radio station was found liable.

Duty. Station took action by putting on the contest.

Act of negligence. Station encouraged listeners to compete among themselves to get there first. An incitement advocates a "clear and imminent danger of some substantive evil which the state constitutionally may seek to prevent."[60] General discussion of the speed laws or advocating raising the speed limits is protected under the First Amendment; inciting people to drive recklessly is not. Provoking thoughtless teenagers under the age of 18–i.e., a class of people lacking contractual capacity–a class of people with an extremely high accident fatality rate–is negligent.

Proximate cause.

Causal connector: But for the contest, the victim would be alive today.

Foreseeability: Station had a large teenage audience and was indeed pitching the contest at them. Teenagers drive cars. Teenagers drive cars recklessly. "[T]he fortuitous absence of prior injury does not justify relieving defendant from responsibility for the foreseeable consequences of its acts."[61]

The *Brandenburg* test–mere advocacy of violence is protected under the First Amendment–is met by inciting the teenagers to act in a dangerous manner and the likelihood that they would act accordingly.

In *Birmingham v. Fodor's Travel Publications, Inc.*,[62] the Supreme Court of Hawaii stopped the plaintiff at the *duty* element. Honeymooning plaintiffs had followed a Fodor's travel guide to Hawaii in selecting a beach and were injured by a dangerous surf. The Court held that a publisher had *no duty to investigate* the beach and warn the readers. In essence, the action of publishing a book was not sufficient to trigger a duty of reasonable care. Only where the publisher takes additional action by guaranteeing the accuracy of the facts contained in the book does the duty arise.[63] It cited *Hanberry v. Hearst Corp.*,[64] as an example where the publisher made an independent examination of a product and gave it a limited express warranty in the form of a "Good Housekeeping's Consumer's Guaranty Seal."

The Court declined to lay a duty of "scrutinizing and even testing all procedures contained in any of their publications."[65] It reasoned that society has a weighty interest in free access to ideas and a negligence duty imposed on publishers would interfere with this to the detriment of all.[66]

It could be generally said that courts in publisher negligence cases have followed the First Amendment protection trend of *New York Times v. Sullivan* in requiring a heightened negligence for liability in the area of publishing. The negligence must be of such an extreme sort that it virtually passes over into the realm of an intentional tort. In the cases of suicide and violence incitement, what is left unanswered, is the question of a vast mass of emotionally unstable fans who are deliberately targeted by publishers, particularly music publishers. Is the situation so very different from tobacco companies who target teenagers knowing that nicotine has addictive qualities? Public opinion has swung heavily against them to hold them the proximate cause of injuries that heretofore we felt were the sole responsibility of the smoker. And on that note, we come to our final area of tort law.

STRICT TORT LIABILITY

Strict Tort or Products Liability is a creation of all fifty state legislatures beginning in the 1960s. *Duty* is imposed by statute on all sellers of products. The effect is to oblige the purchase of products liability insurance so injured consumers will be made whole by some party in the chain of distribution. Strict tort–i.e., liability without a showing of fault–focuses not on negligence but on defects in a product. Thus the manufacturer's "state of the art" defense–I did the best anyone can–is eliminated, and wholesalers and retailers cannot argue the absence of negligence on their part because they were merely a pipeline for the defective goods. The seller is liable "even though he has exercised all possible care in the preparation and sale of the product."[67]

Under products liability law, strict liability is imposed on the theory that " '[t]he costs of damaging events due to defectively dangerous products can best be borne by the enterprisers who make and sell these products.' "[68] The social effect is to oblige all businesses to buy products liability insurance and then pass the cost along to the consumers. Thus the sellers insure the consumers' safety.

Defects are classified as three types: manufacturing, design and failure to warn. A book might have a manufacturing defect through publisher's error, a design defect through the author's error, or a failure to warn the consumer of dangers not readily apparent.

These defects must have the effect of making the product *unreasonably dangerous*. A danger of that level is found by asking if the consumer used the product as safely as possible, is there still an unacceptable risk. The consumer uses the product safely based on knowledge from directions, instructions, warnings, and from the general knowledge of a reasonable person living in the world.[69]

Winter v. G.P. Putnam's Sons[70] was a products liability case involving the *Encyclopedia of Mushrooms*. Relying on the mushroom descriptions in the book, plaintiffs ate toxic species, became critically ill and required liver transplants.

From the plaintiffs' perspective, the elements were obvious:

- *Duty:* imposed by the strict tort statute on all tangible items.
- *Defect:* design–improper description of deadly mushrooms.
- *Unreasonably dangerous:* total ambush through reliance on mushroom expert. Mushroom hunter has no background in the subject, no folk culture, no warning signs on mushrooms themselves–nothing.
- *Proximate cause:* but for the description in the book, plaintiffs would not have eaten the deadly fungus and would have their original livers.

- *Foresee:* totally foreseeable risk on the part of author and publisher.

Nonetheless, the Court refused to expand products liability into the area it described as ideas and expression. The tangible product in a book–the only part subject to strict liability–was the "material and print therein."[71] It drew this line to prevent the inhibition of innovation and to protect those who wished to "share thoughts and theories."[72] It posed the rhetorical question "[w]ith the specter of strict liability, '[w]ould any author wish to be exposed . . . for writing on a topic which might result in physical injury? e.g., *How to cut trees; How to keep bees?*' "[73]

Curiously, a distinction has been made in cases of error in nautical charts with an analogy being drawn between charts and instruments of navigation. " . . . [A]lthough a sheet of paper might not be dangerous, per se, it would be difficult indeed to conceive of a salable commodity with more inherent lethal potential than an aid to aircraft navigation that, contrary to its own design standards, fails to list the highest land mass immediately surrounding a landing site."[74]

In at least one of the chart cases, the exact social allocation language of products liability law is found. "[T]he mass production and marketing of these charts requires Jeppesen to bear the costs of accidents that are proximately caused by defects in the charts . . . "[75]

This, of course, raises the same question that led to Products Liability in the first place. If a product causes injury, shouldn't those who profit from its sale be obliged to charge an adequate price that would cover the liability insurance? If a book is to be used as a guide in hazardous activities–navigating an airplane, picking mushrooms–then doesn't it meet the same tangible standards as an automobile tire? And if the book is dangerously flawed, should it not be driven from the market by the cost of the damages? The courts seem hung up on what are seen as potentially frivolous suits over books on How to Live the Good Life to the point where they are ignoring the books on How to Handle Nitroglycerine Safely.

"A vigorous press, even a 'cantankerous press, an obstinate press, [and] an ubiquitous press' guarantees the flow of information and opinions to the public."[76] One should read "press" to include the entire publishing industry. Nonetheless, the old common law torts provide a significant restraint to protect the citizen. The industry can most likely look to an expansion of the statutorily created strict tort liability as a growth area in that restraint.

NOTES

1. *Bridges v. California*, 314 U.S. 252, 270, 62 S.Ct. 190, 197, 86 L.Ed. 192.
2. *United States v. Associated Press*, 52 F.Supp. 362, 372 (D.C.S.D.N.Y.1943).
3. *Breard v. City of Alexandria*, 341 U.S. 622, 625-626, 71 S.Ct. 920, 923, 95 L.Ed. 1233 (1951).
4. *Time, Inc. v. Hill*, 385 U.S. 374, 410, 87 S.Ct. 534, 17 L.Ed.2d 456, 1 Media L. Rep. 1791.
5. Thus, some of the stronger language of courts on free speech have to be regarded as belonging purely to the context of political debate.

> In the realm of religious faith, and in that of political belief, sharp differences arise. In both fields the tenets of one man may seem the rankest error to his neighbor. To persuade others to his own point of view, the pleader, as we know, at times, resorts to exaggeration, to villification of men who have been, or are, prominent in church or state, and even to false statement. But in spite of the probability of excesses and abuses, these liberties are, in the long view, essential to enlightened opinion and right conduct on the part of the citizens of a democracy. *Cantwell v. Connecticut*, 310 U.S. 296, 310, 60 S.Ct. 900, 906, 84 L.Ed. 1213.

See also *New York Times Co. v. Sullivan* 376 U.S. 254, 272 (citing Mill, *On Liberty* [Oxford: Blackwell, 1947], at 47):

> . . . (T)o argue sophistically, to suppress facts or arguments, to misstate the elements of the case, or misrepresent the opposite opinion . . . all this, even to the most aggravated degree, is so continually done in perfect good faith, by persons who are not considered, and in many other respects may not deserve to be considered, ignorant or incompetent, that it is rarely possible, on adequate grounds, conscientiously to stamp the misrepresentation as morally culpable; and still less could law presume to interfere with this kind of controversial misconduct.

6. *New York Times Co. v. Sullivan*, 376 U.S. 254, 277 (1964).
7. *Rosenbloom v. Metromedia*, 403 U.S. 29, 52-53 (1971).
8. 376 U.S. 254, 84 S.Ct. 710, 11 L.Ed.2d 686 (1964).
9. 376 U.S. at 261.
10. Id. at 269 (citing *Roth v. United States*, 354 U.S. 476, 484, 77 S.Ct. 1304, 1308, 1 L.Ed.2d 1498).
11. Id. (citing *United States v. Associated Press*, 52 F.Supp. 362, 372 [D.C.S.D.N.Y.1943]).
12. Id. at 271.
13. Id. at 280.
14. Id. at 287, 288.
15. *Old Dominion Branch No. 496, Nat'l Ass'n of Letter Carriers v. Austin*, 418 U.S. 264, 281, 94 S.Ct. 2770, 2779, 41 L.Ed.2d 745 (1974).

16. *Gertz v. Robert Welch, Inc.*, 418 U.S. 323 (1974); *Dun & Bradstreet, Inc. v. Greenmoss Builders, Inc.*, 472 U.S. 749, 105 S.Ct. 2939, 86 L.Ed.2d 593 (1985).

17. *Time, Inc. v. Hill*, 385 U.S. 374, 407, 87 S.Ct. 534, 17 L.Ed.2d 456, 1 Media L. Rep. 1791.

18. Id. 385 U.S. at 408.

19. Id. at 389.

20. See, e.g., *Nat'l Treasury Employees Union v. Von Raab*, 489 U.S. 656, 109 S.Ct. 1384, 103 L.Ed. 685 (1989); *Wolf v. People of State of Colorado*, 338 U.S. 25, 28-29, 69 S.Ct. 1359, 1361-1362, 93 L.Ed. 1782 describing immunity from unreasonable search and seizure in right to privacy terms.

21. *Griswold v. Connecticut*, 381 U.S. 479, 85 S.Ct. 1678, 14 L.Ed.2d 510 (1965).

22. Warren and Brandeis, "The Right to Privacy," 4 Harv.L.Rev. 193 (1890).

23. W. Prosser, *Law of Torts*, 831-832 (3d ed. 1964).

24. *Carey v. Brown*, 447 U.S. 455, 100 S.Ct. 2286, 65 L.Ed.2d 263 (1980).

25. *Galella v. Onassis*, 353 F.Supp. 196 (S.D.N.Y.1972), *aff'd in part and rev'd in part*, 487 F.2d 986 (2d Cir.1973).

26. 924 F.Supp. 1413 (1996).

27. Id. at 1417 (citing *Branzburg v. Hays*, 408 U.S. 665, 683, 92 S.Ct. 2646, 2657, 33 L.Ed.2d 626 [1972]).

28. Id. at 1432.

29. Restatement (Second) of Torts § 652B, comment c.

30. See, e.g., *Galella, supra* note 25.

31. 498 F.2d 821.

32. 433 U.S. 562, 97 S.Ct. 2849, 53 L.Ed.2d 965 (1977).

33. 433 U.S. at 578.

34. Id. at 576; *Mazer v. Stein*, 347 U.S. 201, 219, 74 S.Ct. 460, 471, 98 L.Ed. 630 (1954).

35. See, e.g., *Briscoe v. Reader's Digest Association, Inc.*, 4 Cal.3d 529, 543, 93 Cal.Rptr. 866, 483 P.2d 34 (1971).

36. See *Time, Inc. v. Hill*, 385 U.S. at 390-91, 87 S.Ct. at 543- 44.

37. *Galella*, supra note 25.

38. Id. 353 F.Supp. at 216.

39. 128 F.3d 233 (4th Cir., Md.) 1997.

40. Id. at 239.

41. Id. at 251 (citing *Alleco Inc. v. Harry & Jeanette Weinberg Foundation*, 340 Md. 176, 665 A.2d 1038, 1049 [1995] (quoting *Duke v. Feldman*, 245 Md. 454, 226 A.2d 345, 347 [1947]).

42. Id. (citing *Anello v. State*, 201 Md. 164, 93 A.2d 71, 72-73 [Md.1952]).

43. Id. at 241.

44. Id. at 242 (citing *Brandenburg v. Ohio*, 395 U.S. 444, 89 S.Ct. 1827, 23 L.Ed.2d 430 [1969]).

45. It can be found notably in the publication of instructions on making illegal drugs, *United States v. Barnett*, 667 F.2d 835 (9th Cir.1982); aiding and abetting tax fraud, *United States v. Freeman*, 761 F.2d 549, 552-53 (9th Cir.1985), cert. denied, 476 U.S. 1120, 106 S.Ct. 1982, 90 L.Ed.2d 664 (1986); *United States v. Kelley*, 769 F.2d 215 (4th Cir.1985) (defendant participated in preparation of false tax forms by

giving instructions); *United States v. Rowlee*, 899 F.2d 1275 (2d Cir.1990), cert. denied, 498 U.S. 828, 111 S.Ct. 87, 112 L.Ed.2d 59 (1990); *United States v. Moss*, 604 F.2d 569 (8th Cir.1979), cert. denied, 444 U.S. 1071, 100 S.Ct. 1014, 62 L.Ed.2d 752 (1980); *United States v. Buttorff*, 572 F.2d 619, 623-24 (8th Cir.1978) (holding that tax evasion speeches were not subject to *Brandenburg* because although they did not "incite the type of imminent lawless activity referred to in criminal syndicalism cases," they did "go beyond mere advocacy of tax reform"), cert. denied, 437 U.S. 906, 98 S.Ct. 3095, 57 L.Ed.2d 1136 (1978); aiding and abetting in interstate transportation of wager paraphernalia (a computer program), *United States v. Mendelsohn*, 896 F.2d 1183, 1186 (9th Cir. 1990).

46. 128 F.3d 233, 249 (citing *Dennis v. United States*, 341 U.S. 494, 581, 71 S.Ct. 857, 903, 95 L.Ed. 1137 [1951] [Douglas, J., dissenting]).

47. Id. at 262 quoting Plaintiff's brief.

48. Id. at 263.

49. Compare to protected speech: "[The Ku Klux Klan is] not a revengent organization, but if our President, our Congress, our Supreme Court, continues to suppress the white, Caucasian race, it's possible that there might have to be some revengeance taken," *Brandenburg v. Ohio*, 395 U.S. at 444, 446, 89 S.Ct. at 1829; "We'll take the fucking street again," *Hess v. Indiana*, 414 U.S. 105, 108, 94 S.Ct. 326, 328-29, 38 L.Ed.2d 303 (1973); "If we catch any of you going in any of them racist stores, we're gonna break your damn neck," *NAACP v. Claiborne Hardware Co.*, 458 U.S. 886, 902, 102 S.Ct. 3409, 3420, 73 L.Ed.2d 1215 (1982); "If they ever make me carry a rifle the first man I want to get in my sights is L.B.J." *Watts v. United States*, 394 U.S. 705, 706, 89 S.Ct. 1399, 1401, 22 L.Ed.2d 664 (1969).

50. 128 F.3d 233, 265.

51. 249 Cal. Rptr. 187 (Cal. Ct. App. 1988), rev. denied, Oct. 12, 1988.

52. Id. at 190 n.5.

53. *Webster's New Collegiate Dictionary*, G.&C. Merriam Co., 1977.

54. *Brandenburg v. Ohio*, 395 U.S. 444 (1969).

55. *McCollum*, 249 Cal. Rptr. at 193.

56. Id. at 194.

57. Id.

58. See also *Watters v. TSR, Inc.*, 715 F. Supp. 819 (W.D. Ky. 1989) ("Dungeons & Dragons" was not the proximate cause in provoking suicide).

59. 539 P.2d 36, 39 (Cal. 1975).

60. *Whitney v. California*, 274 U.S. 357, 373 (1927).

61. *Weirum*, 539 P.2d at 40.

62. 73 Haw. 359, 833 P.2d 70 (Haw. 1992).

63. 73 Haw. at 366.

64. 276 Cal.App.2d 680, 683-84, Cal.Rptr. 519, 521 (1969).

65. 73 Haw. at 368.

66. Id. at 369.

67. *Restatement (Second) of Torts* § 402A (1964).

68. W. Page Keeton et al., *Prosser and Keeton on the Law of Torts* 98, at 92-93 (5th ed. 1984).

69. See, e.g., *Walter v. Bauer*, 439 N.Y.S.2d 821, 823 (Sup. Ct. 1981) (student injured following science experiment described in textbook does not have a cause of action–defective design and failure to warn–against the publisher based on a theory of products liability), aff'd in part & rev'd in part on other grounds, 451 N.Y.S.2d 533 (App. Div. 1982).

70. 938 F.2d 1033 (9th Cir. 1991).

71. Id. at 1034.

72. Id. at 1035.

73. Id. (citing *Walter v. Bauer*, 109 Misc.2d 189, 191, 439 N.Y.S.2d 821, 823 [Sup.Ct.1981]).

74. *Fluor Corp. v. Jeppesen & Co.*, 170 Cal.App.3d 468, 475-76, 216 Cal.Rptr. 68, 71-72 (1985).

75. *Aetna Casualty and Surety Co. v. Jeppesen & Co.*, 642 F.2d 339, 341-42 (9th Cir. 1981).

76. *Wolfson v. Lewis*, 924 F.Supp. 1413, 1416 (citing *United States v. New York Times Co.*, 328 F.Supp. 324, 331 [S.D.N.Y.], rev'd, 444 F.2d 544 [2d Cir. 1971] [en banc], rev'd 403 U.S. 713, 91 S.Ct. 2140, 29 L.Ed.2d 822 [1971] [per curiam]).

ANTI-TRUST

The Publishing Merger That Failed: Reed Elsevier and Wolters Kluwer

William M. Hannay

What was billed a year ago as the largest merger in publications industry history collapsed in early 1998, a victim of its overblown scale and the antitrust concerns it raised. This paper describes the nature of the proposed merger, the background of U.S. antitrust law and European Community competition law in which it was analyzed, and the specific antitrust problems perceived by the government enforcement agencies. In doing so, some predictions about the reaction of enforcers to future convergence in the publishing industry may be made.

William Hannay is the head of the Antitrust Practice Group and a partner in the Chicago-based law firm, Schiff, Hardin & Waite. A regular speaker at the Charleston Conference, he is also Adjunct Professor at IIT/Chicago-Kent College of Law.

[Haworth co-indexing entry note]: "The Publishing Merger That Failed: Reed Elsevier and Wolters Kluwer." Hannay, William M. Co-published simultaneously in *The Acquisitions Librarian* (The Haworth Information Press, an imprint of The Haworth Press, Inc.) No. 26, 2001, pp. 173-179; and: *Publishing and the Law: Current Legal Issues* (ed: A. Bruce Strauch) The Haworth Information Press, an imprint of The Haworth Press, Inc., 2001, pp. 173-179. Single or multiple copies of this article are available for a fee from The Haworth Document Delivery Service [1-800-342-9678, 9:00 a.m. - 5:00 p.m. (EST). E-mail address: getinfo@haworthpressinc.com].

173

THE NATURE OF THE PROPOSED MERGER

Last October, two publishing giants–the British-Dutch enterprise Reed Elsevier PLC and the Dutch-owned company Wolters Kluwer N.V.–announced their intention to merge. Under the proposed arrangement, a new entity called Elsevier Wolters Kluwer would have been formed. Wolters Kluwer's stockholders would have received a 27.5% share of the new company, valued at about $ 8.8 billion, while Reed PLC and Elsevier N.V. shareholders would have received 38.3% and 34.2% shares, respectively.

Ironically, this was the second time around for the parties. Ten years earlier, Elsevier had attempted a hostile takeover of Kluwer, which escaped by running to the arms of a "white knight," Wolters Sampson. A few years later, Elsevier merged with Reed International. In 1996, Kluwer acquired Little Brown & Co., publisher of print and electronic legal materials that yield about $25 million in annual sales. That company, which has now been folded into Aspen Publishing, acquired the law division of John Wiley & Sons in November.

Then came the proposed merger to acquire Wolters Kluwer.

After the deal was announced, analysts described it as a good fit for both companies because it would couple Reed's many primary publications and its online database LEXIS-NEXIS with Kluwer's secondary materials, including its CD-ROMs. They noted that few of the two companies' titles compete head to head. Had it gone through, however, the merger would have significantly increased concentration in the professional publishing industry. In the worldwide legal publishing market, for example, a Reed Elsevier-Wolters Kluwer conglomerate would have become a muscle-bound giant with some $2.3 billion in revenues, nearly double that of its nearest competitor, the Thomson Corp.

The proposed merger raised concerns among those already unhappy with the earlier West-Thompson merger, according to an article in the January 1998 *ABA Journal.* In the article, Kendall F. Svengalis, chief law librarian of Rhode Island, described the West-Thompson merger as follows: "It has been disastrous for publicly funded law libraries," many of which are suffering budget cuts while prices soar. "The price increase for legal publications is three times what the increase in my budget has been," he says. "It has caused the librarians to rethink their collections." The ABA article also cited the comments of Judy Meadows, president of the American Association of Law Librarians, who noted that the Reed Elsevier-Wolters Kluwer consolidation troubles many law librarians, who fear reduced competition will lead to a reduction in the number of legal resources and an increase in prices.

A combined Reed Elsevier and Wolters Kluwer would also have created a giant in the scientific publishing industry, where Elsevier Science is the overwhelming market leader with more than $850 million in U.S. scientific revenues alone. Adding in Wolters Kluwer's $235 million in U.S. scientific revenues, the merged company would again have significantly overshadowed its nearest competitor, the Thomson Corp., which has only about $200 million in U.S. revenues.

THE LEGAL BACKGROUND: U.S. ANTITRUST LAW

In 1914, Congress enacted the Clayton Act as an "incipiency" statute, intended to reach particular types of practices *before* competition is harmed. Section 7 of the Clayton Act (15 U.S.C. § 18) prohibits any acquisition of stock or assets whose effect "may be substantially to lessen competition, or to tend to create a monopoly" in any line of commerce. Government enforcement of Section 7 is facilitated by the Hart-Scott-Rodino Act (15 U.S.C. § 18A). This statute requires the parties to large acquisitions and mergers to provide advance notice to the Federal Trade Commission and the Justice Department (so-called "premerger notification") before they can complete the transaction.

In interpreting Section 7, courts have traditionally given the statute's "may be" language a broadly prophylactic reading, tipping the scale against mergers in close questions. Over the past 25 years, federal and state governments have struggled to articulate the proper legal criteria to use in determining whether an acquisition violates Section 7 and have periodically issued "guidelines" setting forth the results of their efforts. While not binding on courts, these guidelines shape the decision-making of the agencies and are, in this sense, often result determinative. The most current statement of Department of Justice and Federal Trade Commission policy on horizontal mergers was issued jointly in 1992. *See* Horizontal Merger Guidelines of 1992, 4 Trade Reg. Rep. (CCH) ¶ 13,104 (1992).

With respect to mergers between competitors (such as the proposed publishing merger), the "unifying theme" of the Guidelines is that "mergers should not be permitted to create or enhance market power or to facilitate its exercise," market power being defined as the ability to maintain a selling price above competitive levels. In applying the Guidelines, an enforcement agency assesses whether the merger would significantly increase concentration in the relevant market or markets and, if so, whether the merger, in light of market concentration and other factors that characterize the market, raises concern about potential adverse competitive effects. As part of this assessment, the agency will consider whether subsequent entry by one or more potential competitors would be "timely, likely and sufficient" either to deter or to counteract the competitive effects of the merger.

THE LEGAL BACKGROUND: EU COMPETITION LAW

European Union competition law started from quite a different perspective than America's. When the Treaty of Rome was signed in 1957, Community integration was the dominant goal. *See* Treaty Establishing the European Economic Community (1957), 298 U.N.T.S. 11. Unlike American antitrust policy, the EU's original competition policy reflected a favorable attitude toward concentrations and government regulation. Substantive economic and anticompetitive analysis largely did not exist. Things began to change in the 1980s.

In 1989, the EU adopted the Merger Regulation which prohibits concentrations that create or enhance a "dominant position" so as to impede effective competition. *See* Commission Regulation 4064/89 of Dec. 21, 1989. The EU Merger Regulation embodies a "one-stop shopping" policy, i.e., most transactions that fall within its terms are governed exclusively by the Merger Regulation, and not by national laws of EU Member States.

The Merger Regulation requires prior notification of proposed "concentrations" within its scope to the Competition Directorate (DG-IV) of the European Commission. Transactions may not be consummated until a required waiting period has elapsed or the Commission has acted. "Concentrations" include acquisitions, mergers, and "concentrative" joint ventures. The Regulation applies to all concentrations with a "Community dimension," which is defined as transactions that meet certain financial thresholds set out in Article 1(2). Because these thresholds are quite high, however, relatively few concentrations are notified to the Commission.

Under Article 2(3), a "concentration" that "creates or strengthens a dominant position as a result of which effective competition would be significantly impeded in the common market or in a substantial part of it" is deemed incompatible with the common market and therefore prohibited. In applying this test, the Commission "must place its appraisal within the general framework of the achievement of the fundamental objectives referred to in Article 2 of the Treaty, including that of strengthening the Community's economic and social cohesion." *See* Recital 13 of the Regulation. Transactions resulting in a market share of less than 25% are likely to be deemed not to impede effective competition and, therefore, to be compatible with the common market.

THE REACTION OF GOVERNMENT ENFORCERS

On November 10, 1997, Reed Elsevier and Wolters Kluwer formally notified the European Commission of their intention to merge. Objections to the merger were in turn filed by several organizations and competitors. For example, Nederlandse Federatie van Belastingadviseurs, a body representing Dutch tax consultants, and law publisher KSU filed objections both with the Ministry of Economic Affairs in The Netherlands and with the European Commissioner for Competition (DG-IV).

On December 11th, the European Commission decided to open an in-depth investigation of the merger, because of its implications for competition in a number of national markets for professional publishing. The Commission was of the preliminary view that the merger between these two leading publishers could create a dominant position in several "markets," some quite large and some quite small:

- in the world-wide market for academic publishing (scientific journals and books),
- in the markets for publications for professional use in the areas of law and tax in The Netherlands, in the United Kingdom, in France and in Italy,
- in the market for publications for primary and secondary schools (educational publishing) in the United Kingdom,
- in a number of markets for business publications in The Netherlands,
- in the market for Dutch dictionaries, and

- in the European market for the services provided by transport databases.

Following an in-depth inquiry, the Commission confirmed its objections on competition grounds in a statement to Wolters Kluwer and Reed Elsevier on February, 2, 1998. A month later, on March 9, 1998, the two companies announced that they had decided to abandon the merger.

In a joint statement, the two companies said that "Wolters Kluwer has made it known to Reed Elsevier that it needed to renegotiate a number of the terms of the proposed merger." European Commission approval for the deal would have required divestitures by Wolters that jeopardised the 15% earnings per share estimate given to shareholders in October. Wolters demanded 30% of the combined group compared with the 27.50% initially agreed. When Reed refused to renegotiate, the merger fell apart.

In a press release issued on March 11th, the European Commission described in greater detail the concerns that it had about the proposed merger, as follows:

> [T]he enquiry . . . led the Commission to consider that the position of the merged entity, several times larger than any other publisher of professional information in the EU, could prevent a competitive situation in the supply of legal, fiscal and scientific information in the EU, with a significant impact on the terms and prices at which this information is made available to user and consumers. The merger as notified, could also affect the development of a competitive environment in the supply of professional information in electronic form. The combination of the parties' financial resources and ownership of copyrighted content across Europe would discourage investments by competitors in this area.

SUBSEQUENT EVENTS

Less than two months after the proposed merger fell through, Reed Elsevier announced that it had agreed to acquire two legal publishers from Times Mirror Co. for $1.65 billion. If the new deal is consummated, Reed Elsevier would add to its lists both Matthew Bender & Co. and the remaining 50% interest that it did not already own in

Shepard's Co., a database of legal citations that it has operated in partnership with Times Mirror since 1996. By contrast with the failed merger, the acquisition from Times Mirror seems like small potatoes, neither as large nor as dramatic. To that degree, it is less likely to incur the wrath of EU enforcers. However, the American enforcers, who were remarkably silent about the prior merger, may become more interested in this one.

Antitrust Update:
The Robinson-Patman Act Rides Again and Mergers Come Under Increased Scrutiny

Glen M. Secor

INTRODUCTION

Antitrust issues have dominated the business news of late. But while others are fixated on the Microsoft showdown with the Department of Justice ("DOJ"), the book industry need look no further than its own borders (or, as discussed below, Borders) for hot antitrust battles.

Publishing/book industry antitrust matters, including those playing out now, generally fall into two categories: (1) Pricing discrimination; or, (2) Anti-competitive impact of a merger or acquisition. The first category, pricing discrimination (under the Robinson-Patman Act) is perhaps the most familiar to us in the book industry, given the prominence in recent years of investigations by the Federal Trade Commission ("FTC" or "Commission") (a division of the DOJ) and American Booksellers Association ("ABA") lawsuits involving publisher pricing practices.[1] Having successfully settled Robinson-Patman suits against six publishers, the ABA has most recently turned its attention to the

Glen M. Secor is President, Yankee Book Peddler, Inc., 999 Maple Street, Contoocook, NH 03229.

[Haworth co-indexing entry note]: "Antitrust Update: The Robinson-Patman Act Rides Again and Mergers Come Under Increased Scrutiny." Secor, Glen M. Co-published simultaneously in *The Acquisitions Librarian* (The Haworth Information Press, an imprint of The Haworth Press, Inc.) No. 26, 2001, pp. 181-188; and: *Publishing and the Law: Current Legal Issues* (ed: A. Bruce Strauch) The Haworth Information Press, an imprint of The Haworth Press, Inc., 2001, pp. 181-188. Single or multiple copies of this article are available for a fee from The Haworth Document Delivery Service [1-800-342-9678, 9:00 a.m. - 5:00 p.m. (EST). E-mail address: getinfo@haworthpressinc.com].

181

buying practices of the major chains, bringing suit against Barnes & Noble ("B&N") and Borders for alleged Robinson-Patman violations.[2]

The second major category of publishing antitrust concerns, anticompetitive or monopolistic effects of mergers and acquisitions, is governed by the Clayton Act (Section 7) and the Sherman Act (Section 2).[3] A detailed discussion of these laws and their impact on publishing mergers is outside the scope of this article, but this area bears watching as the global publishing industry continues to reshape itself.

Publishing has generally been a very competitive industry, with numerous publishers supplying and vying for any given market. But consolidation in the industry, including the rise of the global superpublisher (e.g., Bertelsmann, Reed Elsevier et al.), has changed the competitive landscape and opened up the possibility of market domination. Not surprisingly, then, we have seen a number of mergers and proposed mergers come under antitrust investigation or challenge, including Thomson/West,[4] the abandoned Reed Elsevier/Wolters Kluwer merger (sunk, essentially, by European Union antitrust concerns),[5] and, most recently, Bertelsmann/Random House.[6]

The focus of this article, though, is on Robinson-Patman actions concerning illegal pricing discrimination. Special attention is paid to the specifics of the recently filed ABA complaint against B&N and Borders.

OVERVIEW OF ROBINSON-PATMAN

The Robinson-Patman Act ("RPA") was passed in 1936, as an amendment to Section 2 of the Clayton Act. When we talk about Robinson-Patman, then, we are talking about Section 2 of the Clayton Act, as amended by the Robinson-Patman Act. Robinson-Patman prohibits six different categories of price discrimination, as defined by the following subsections:

- Section 2(a) prohibits discrimination in price for goods of "like grade and quality" resulting in competitive injury, unless the discrimination is cost justified.
- Section 2(b) places the burden of proof (rebuttal) on the defendant upon the showing of a prima facie case of discrimination; also sets out a defense for price discrimination "made in good faith to meet an equally low price of a competitor."

- Section 2(c) prohibits brokerage fees and similar payments to buyers except for actual services rendered by the buyer.
- Section 2(d) prohibits sellers from paying for buyer processing and handling services, unless such services are available to competing buyers "on proportionally equal terms."
- Section 2(e) prohibits sellers from providing services or facilities to buyers, except where such services or facilities are available to competing buyers "on proportionally equal terms."
- Section 2(f) prohibits *buyers* from *inducing* or *receiving* the types of discriminatory pricing covered by Sections 2(a)-2(e).[7]

PREVIOUS ROBINSON-PATMAN ACTIONS

In 1988, the FTC issued administrative complaints, alleging violation of Sections 2(a), 2(d), and 2(e) of the RPA, against Harper & Row, Macmillan, Hearst (Morrow), Putnam Berkeley, Simon & Schuster, and Random House. The FTC dismissed those complaints in 1996, citing "significant events that have occurred in the industry since the complaints were issued–including the initiation of private litigation addressing many of the same issues" and concluding that further investigation would not merit the time and public resources required.[8]

The "private litigation" to which the Commission refers was, of course, the suits against individual publishers brought by the ABA. Since the Robinson-Patman claims asserted by the FTC and the ABA in their respective complaints were similar, and since the ABA suits had been settled, the Commission was essentially able to defer any remaining issues to the courts. [Note: though not legally binding in and of themselves, the ABA has promulgated "Rules for the Application of the Robinson-Patman Act to Book Publishing," covering both "price discrimination" and "promotional allowance discrimination."][9]

In its Dismissal Order, the Commission noted that, between 1988 and 1996, "the dynamics and structure of the book distribution market have evolved in significant ways, reflecting the growth of 'superstores' and warehouse or 'club' stores." It is interesting to see the trend towards superstores cited in support of dismissal of the claims, since most superstores are owned by the major chains and differential pricing for chains and independents is at the heart of the ABA lawsuits.

More to the point, the Commission also noted that publishers had replaced the allegedly illegal pricing practices–"unjustified quantity discounts on trade books and secret discounts on mass market books"–with "other pricing strategies."

INDEPENDENTS VS. NATIONAL CHAINS: THE ABA TAKES ON BARNES & NOBLE AND BORDERS

Apparently some of the existing pricing practices still vex independent booksellers, as evidenced by the recent suit filed by the ABA on behalf of 26 independent bookstores against Barnes & Noble and Borders for RPA Section 2(f) violations. Recall that Sec. 2(f) deals with *buyer* conduct. The ABA complaint, filed 18 March 98 in U.S. District Court for the Northern District of California, provides a litany of alleged illegal buying practices by the chains and sets out the RPA battle lines between the independents and the chains.[10]

In its complaint against B&N and Borders, the ABA charges violation of the RPA, the California Unfair Trade Practices Act, and the California Unfair Competition Law. Relief sought includes injunctive and declaratory relief, treble damages (a significant feature of RPA actions), disgorgement of illicit gains received in California since 18 March 94 (coinciding, apparently, with a four-year Statute of Limitations for the claims brought), and attorney fees. The suit alleges that B&N and Borders, through "secret and illegal deals," are "driving independent bookstores out of business . . . across the country." Citing the explosion of superstores between 1992 and 1997 (from 135 to 469 and 31 to 189 for B&N and Borders, respectively), the complainants assert that the chains use their "enormous leverage to obtain secret and illegal deals from their captive suppliers."

In its RPA claim, the ABA alleges that B&N and Borders have "solicited, induced and received" numerous pricing advantages which are unavailable to independent bookstores. These include:

- "Off schedule" discounts in excess of publisher stated discounts for highest volume purchasers.
- Special deals with retail distribution centers owned and operated by publisher.
- "Shared markdowns" on unsold retailer inventory. These are additional discounts on unsold bookstore copies, which "effec-

tively reward defendants for purchasing titles in quantities they cannot sell, and competitively disadvantage independent bookstores that have purchased appropriate levels of inventory."

- Extra discounts on small orders.
- Special pricing terms for new stores or expansions. The complaint cites an instance in which Borders unilaterally took an additional three percent (3%) "allowance" (i.e., discount) and demanded free freight for all back orders.
- Incentive payments or additional discount based on "sell through" . . . total purchases, or other factors.
- "Special pricing terms based on the returnable nature of the sales." These are allowances paid or deductions taken when books are returned or even on the basis of anticipated future returns.
- Special terms for nonreturnable purchases.
- "Purported shortage discounts," i.e., deductions beyond the amount of actual short shipments.
- Unilateral write-offs or write-downs of amounts owed the publisher by the chains.
- A variety of abuses relating to promotional payments and co-op advertising, including pricing reductions disguised as promotional payments, promotional payments in excess of any actual promotional work done by the defendants, and payment for "featuring" titles in the stores. This latter category allegedly includes window displays, face-out display, end of aisle display, and inclusion in "programs such as 'Discover New Writers' or 'New Arrivals'."

The crux of the Robinson-Patman claim, of course, is not that these special pricing deals are made, but rather that they are offered on a discriminatory basis and are not generally available to independent bookstores. One might wonder, though, given the results of the ABA suits against publishers, how such price discrimination can continue to exist. After all, the alleged illegal pricing terms are coming *from* the publishers. According to the portrait painted in the ABA's complaint, the industry dynamic has shifted (or shifted further) in the big chains' favor. According to one publishing executive quoted (anonymously) in the complaint, "Part of the problem is that we're scared of them. If they don't like our terms of sale, they threaten not to buy books, which can substantially hurt our relationship with authors and agents."

These strong-arming tactics of B&N and Borders and their yield of favorable pricing terms, according to the ABA, is part of an aggressive growth strategy intended to saturate key geographic markets and drive out independent bookstores. Through this strategy, again according to the ABA, the big chains have succeeded in grabbing market share, but often at the cost of corporate profits. The suit alleges that the chains have truly saturated the retail book market and that new and expanded stores would be unprofitable without these "illicit deals." Indeed, the plaintiffs claim, "even the limited profits resulting from defendants' massive growth strategies over the past five years have been aided in significant part by secret deals that are unlawful." One option to improve profitability would be to reduce price competition at the retail level, which B&N and Borders will be better able to do as they become increasingly dominant in the market.

Armed with their illegal pricing advantages, the ABA claims, the national chains have targeted certain key markets and, in one cited instance, at least, a specific bookstore.[11] The resulting competitive disadvantage for independent bookstores has led to a forty percent decline in the national market share of independent bookstores since 1991 and "countless" independent bookstore failures. The "ultimate victims" of this trend, the complaint states, "will not only be the many independent bookstores forced out of business, but also the book reading public." In addition to the oft-cited loss of personal service and choice, the ABA also asserts that consumers do not do as well economically as one might think through retail price competition–publishers make up the revenue lost through increased discounts by raising the list prices.

We've only heard thus far from one side in this dispute. The ABA's claims, if true, would certainly indicate Robinson-Patman Sec. 2(f) violations. One would expect the responses of B&N and Borders to address not only the specific practices alleged in the complaint, but also the broader business and economic dynamics of bookselling in the late 1990s. For example, what is the market and who are the competitors for B&N and Borders? If on-line booksellers and book clubs are included in the analysis, particularly in the global context, how is the anti-competitiveness equation affected? Does a "meeting the competition" defense emerge from a broader definition of the "book market"?

These questions are asked out of curiosity and not in support of answers going one way or the other. If the practices alleged in the ABA's complaint are proved and if those "special" terms are not available to other booksellers, B&N and Borders will have difficulty avoiding a finding of RPA Sec. 2(f) violations. This type of differential pricing, if not justified by cost or competitive necessity, and whether overt or hidden, seems to fall squarely within the issues and principles addressed in prior ABA suits against publishers. If so, we should expect to see the practices in question stopped by settlement(s) or judgment(s).

CONCLUSION

The book industry, in the U.S. and globally, is undergoing a number of wrenching changes. Market consolidation among publishers and booksellers is redefining the competitive dynamic of the entire book industry. Market dominance or the threat of market dominance is at the heart of book industry antitrust concerns. Robinson-Patman pricing discrimination actions continue hot and heavy, while the specter of the Clayton Act looms ever larger in publishing mergers and acquisitions.

NOTES

1. See "FTC Drops R-P Act Book Publishing Proceeding on Public Interest Grounds," *BNA Antitrust and Trade Regulation Report,* v. 71, no. 1780, p. 277, 26 Sep 96 (discussing the end of the proceedings begun in 1988 against Harper & Row, Macmillan, Hearst (Morrow), Putnam Berkeley, Simon & Schuster, and Random House); "ABA Settles with St. Martin's: Random House Suit Proceeds," *Bookweb: Bookselling this Week,* 19 Aug 96, http://www.bookweb.org/news/btw (archives) (announcing the final settlement stemming from suits filed against five publishers in May 1994 (St. Martin's, Hugh Lauter Levin, Houghton Mifflin, Penguin USA, and Rutledge Hill); "Random House Settles," *Bookweb: Bookselling this Week,* Nov 96, www.bookweb.org/news/btw (archives).

2. See "Wow. ABA Sues Barnes & Noble and Borders," *PW Daily for Booksellers,* 18 Mar 98, email: pwdailybook@soapbox.bookwire.com.

3. See Perle, E. Gabriel and John Taylor Williams, *The Publishing Law Handbook, 2d ed.,* § 10.02. Section 2 of the Sherman Act prohibits monopolies and attempts to monopolize in interstate commerce. Section 7 of the Clayton Act prohibits mergers and acquisitions which serve "substantially to lessen competition or to tend to create a monopoly."

4. See Hannay, William M., "Go West, Young Thomson!," *Against the Grain,* Dec 97-Jan 98, p. 42 (discussing pre-merger objections raised by law librarians, competing publishers, and various states' attorneys general to the acquisition of West by Thomson).

5. See "Proposed Reed Elsevier/Wolters Kluwer Merger Abandoned," *Information Today,* Apr 98, p. 1 (the parties abandoned the proposed merger rather than undertake the divestitures which would likely have been required by the European Commission).

6. See "Authors, Agents Challenge Random/BDD Merger," *Publishers Weekly,* 27 Apr 98, p. 10; "Bertelsmann Unfazed by Antitrust Concerns," *Subtext* On-line, 26 Mar 98; "FTC Bump: Bertelsmann Withdraws/Resubmits Application," *PW Daily for Booksellers,* 4 May 98.

7. See *Antitrust Trade Laws and Regulation, Chapter 4: The Robinson-Patman Act,* Matthew Bender & Co. (1997).

8. See Donald S. Clark, "The Robinson-Patman Act: Annual Update," a speech before the Robinson-Patman Act Committee Section of Antitrust Law delivered 2 Apr 98, http://www.ftc.gov/speeches/other/spring98.htm. Mr. Clark is Secretary of the FTC.

9. The rules can be found at http://www.ambook.org/bookweb/btw/103095/art1a.html.

10. A copy of the complaint can be found at http://www.bookweb.org/pressroom.

11. In this incident, B&N employees in Missoula, Montana, were allegedly told that "the corporation's success in Missoula would be measured by whether one of the leading independent bookstores in the community was put out of business."

Index

For Product Safety Concerns and Information please contact our EU representative GPSR@taylorandfrancis.com Taylor & Francis Verlag GmbH, Kaufingerstraße 24, 80331 München, Germany

T - #0044 - 270225 - C0 - 212/152/12 [14] - CB - 9780789007773 - Gloss Lamination